# WOMEN LIKE ME

Stories of Resilience and Courage

## JULIE FAIRHURST

Rock Star Publishing

The authors of this book do not dispense medical advice or prescribe the use of any technique as a form of treatment for physical, emotional, or medical problems without a physician's advice, either directly or indirectly. The authors intend to provide general information to individuals who are taking positive steps in their lives for emotional and spiritual well-being. If you use any information in this book for yourself, which is your constitutional right, the authors and the publisher assume no responsibility for your actions.

"Strong women aren't simply born. We are forged through the challenges of life. With each challenge, we grow mentally and emotionally. We move forward with our head held high and a strength that can not be denied. A woman who's been through the storm and survived. We are warriors."

**UNKNOWN**

# Contents

Memories of Margaret (Dolly) Ann Yavis     1

Introduction     5

1. Everybody Dies     9
2. Tales From an Expert Former Hider     19
3. The Cabin in the Woods     27
4. Day Zero     39
5. A Love Letter to Myself     53
6. Own Your Life to Become Finally Free     61
7. How I became the Mom to Moms     81
8. Finding Your Inner Power     89
9. The Journey of Voice Awakening     99
10. I'll Never Be Like Them     109
11. Abandoned     127
12. How My Mirror Saved My Life     133
13. Meet the Authors     139
14. Meet Julie Fairhurst     153

Other Books by Julie Fairhurst     157

Acknowledgments     159

Want to be a Women Like Me Author?     163

*I am dedicating this volume of Women Like Me to GG (Grandmother) Dolly Yavis. Dolly left us in 2021 at the age of 95. She will be forever missed.*

*We are so lucky when our elder family members stay with us for many years. My grandparents passed away when I was in my 20's. GG is my husband's grandmother. He and his other family members were so fortunate to have the time to spend with Dolly. I, too, was grateful for my time with her.*

*How many of you have grandparents that are still with you? If you do, I hope you take the time to visit with them and ask questions about their lives. Imagine the changes in our world that GG saw from 1925 to 2021. She lived in a few different worlds on earth. It must have been an extraordinary life to see all the advancements with technology.*

*What about your senior family members? Do you know what it was like for them? Have you ever asked about their loves and losses, successes and failures, hopes, dreams, and achievements in their lives?*

*Once they leave this world, you no longer have the opportunity to ask questions. Family members try to remember, but their memories will fade, and you may never know what an amazing life they lived.*

*I encourage you to visit your loved ones, ask them about their lives. Ask them about their secrets (we all have them). They might open up and share their life stories with you.*

*And maybe you can write it all down and one day tell the story of your elders who leave you. Then you can share their life with younger family members, so they are never forgotten.*

*GG, you will be missed but never forgotten.*

*Julie*

## Memories of Margaret (Dolly) Ann Yavis

1925 - 2021

Possibly her beginnings made her the way she was – refreshing and effervescent, like a bottle of good champagne had just been popped whenever she entered a room or gathering.

Born at the end of June, in Regina, at the height of their rainy season, and 1925 was no exception; in fact, it rained so much just a few days after she was born, on the 28th of that blustery month, it held a quarter century's daily rain record.

She bragged to us as a child of walking to school in knee-deep snow worsened by double-digit below zero temperatures in either scale of counting. Summers, she swam in ponds, lakes, and streams before any swimming pools became the norm. At four years old, she would have been oblivious to the Great Depression's beginnings, but when the Dust Bowl's drought began a few years later, it left Canada's financial, industrial, and agriculture sectors in tatters creating a decade long financial collapse, not even a child could mistake for the norm. Things once taken for granted would no longer be there.

At fourteen, circumstances dictated she had to go and live with her mother's brother's family in Drumheller, Alberta. They were weathering the economic storm better than others in Canada, and they had room available in their comfortable, homey house. If there were oases in Canada's bleak decade, Drumheller was one of them. A new railway junction, large coal reserves, and recent oil discoveries added to its international mystique as the Badlands. Its unique moniker became synonymous with dinosaur fossils that brought university teams from around the world to dig, sift, crate, and haul out.

Was it coming from nothing, and then having something again that molded her soul's essence? Or did her future father-in-law set an example when he told his restaurant staff and their home's domestic helper never to deny any transient jobless man a meal? Or did they reinforce each other in one of life's best examples of learning?

Married at nineteen, it should have been the beginning of a prosperous life, but like before, fate had more in store for this young couple. The consequences of untimely family deaths had created unknowns where there should have been knowns which created gypsy-like ramblings as they created four more lives. British Columbia's coast lured them after giving up on Alberta. They heard life was easier in BC.

Lower Mainland in 1959: apples were there for the picking, all you needed to eat salmon was a fishhook, and the climate rarely slipped more than a degree or two below freezing.

Those enticements couldn't be denied. They arrived separately in BC; mom and the three youngest children came by train, and father and I in a 1950 Chevrolet sedan delivery several days later. Dad had stopped in the Okanagan and picked up some apples, and when they first greeted each other, his first words were, "I have the apples," and mom beamingly replied, "I have the salmon." as she fetched several jars of canned salmon she had been gifted.

In BC, having zero dollars was a flight up from where they were in zero's basement. What money they did have was owed to family and friends, but they had one thing to their advantage – time and the audacity of youth. Time to get their first fledgling restaurant up and running, before house or home were thought of. We lived in the crowded simplest of accommodations in the back of the restaurant until all debts were paid before finally moving into an actual house almost two years later.

This is where Dolly really shone. No matter the adversity, her smile never waned. True, there were many more trials and challenges, but as her children grew and exasperated those challenges to new levels, one thing never changed – mom's mood! True, she could momentarily become angry, frustrated, or both if confronted with outlandish stupidity, but she was never moody!

She was always the person to go to when your life needed some picking up. Her door was always open, and her welcoming smile was always genuine and warm. As important, your hunger pangs were always satiated within minutes of opening that door, no matter the time. You would soon be seated at her table with a variety of choices to either nibble at or to wolf down.

Similarly, all her children's friends were treated like family even in the most awkward of times. On more than one Thanksgiving or Christmas dinner, I remember the table being quickly rearranged to sit unexpected friends or long-lost relatives who were doing without. At other more delicate times, she would offer breakfast and not admonishments.

That is not to say she was anyone's fool, but she was a master of timing – there was a time to do what needed to be done and another time to talk about it. The epitome of grace – she literally owned that word and displayed it proudly.

**Jamie Yavis**

"I wish that more women realized that helping another woman win, cheering her on, praying for her, or sharing a resource with her does not take away from the blessings coming to them. In fact, the more you give, the more you receive. Empowering women doesn't come from selfishness but rather from selflessness."

**SELENE KINDER**

# Introduction

JULIE FAIRHURST

We can heal through telling our stories. That healing can also be passed onto the reader, who may gain insight, courage, and acceptance through reading another woman's story.

We all have stories, every one of us. Our stories are what define us and the life we live. Our past experiences will shape our lives, sometimes for the good and sometimes for the bad. When we experience trauma, insecurity, loss, confusion, and feelings of unworthiness, it won't be easy to live our best lives.

Research shows that writing about our past events can have favorable benefits on the writer's emotional and physical health. Release can come by being able to release any negativity surrounding the emotions of your story. This can happen when you put pen to paper and let your story out of your head and your heart onto paper.

I know for many women myself included, opening up and telling our story will bring clarity to our lives. And it will allow us to not live in shame or guilt. Shame and guilt are dangerous emotions that hold us back, kill our self-esteem and the dreams we have for ourselves and our families. When women tell their stories, when they write them down, and when they are willing to go past the shame and guilt they may be feeling and share their stories with the world, they will be able to start living their best lives.

We all know that holding onto events that cause us to want to hide and feel shameful eventually will cause us great harm. Not just to our self-esteem and confidence but our physical health as well. This is why women must gain some distance from their emotions. Gaining a clearer understanding of why you feel the way you do and how those feelings impact you is vital to your well-being. Women find it impossible to see the big picture for their lives when hiding deep inside themselves.

Writing your story, even a short one, can seem in the beginning to be a daunting task. Many of the writers have almost quit, feeling it was too much. When we relive the past, triggers and emotions pushed down for many years could rise to the surface. These are brave women who write in Women Like Me.

The women writers in this book write about experiences that are important to tell. We learn from telling each other stories. The women in the book learn more about themselves by writing their stories, but they hope to help other women who may feel similar feelings or have similar experiences.

Knowing that they may help others in some way by telling their stories gave them the courage and motivation to get their story out and into this book for all to read.

As you go on and read the stories of these incredible women; please remember what you've read here and how difficult it may have been for them to put their story on paper and into this book. And remember, they didn't just do it for themselves. They did it for you as well. So we can all live our best life.

As the reader, I hope you will find comfort and healing from the stories that are told.

"We'll be friends forever, won't
we, Pooh?" asked Piglet. "Even
longer." Pooh answered."

**WINNIE THE POOH**

# ONE

## Everybody Dies

### BUT TODAY IS NOT MY DAY

At first glance, most people would probably say I had a privileged childhood. I grew up on the West Side of Vancouver, B.C., on First and Dunbar, a couple of blocks from the beach. My playground was Jericho Beach, and I was given all the freedom a child of that era could ask for. I rode my bike down to the beach with my friends and played until it was dinner time, and then went home. I went to a private school from midway through Grade 3 to Grade 12 because my parents were unsatisfied with the public school system. I was a shy child, so moving to a new school halfway through Grade 3 was traumatizing, and I was unhappy for months. I have one younger sister who annoyed me back then because she always wanted to tag along to all my events and activities. It's funny how relationships with family change over the years. I love her now with all my heart and could not function properly without her in my life.

On the outside, I had a wonderful life, but it was not all rosy and happy. We had secrets, just like any family. I would never say that my mother was a terrible mother, and she did the best that she could with the tools that life had given her. I still have difficulty comprehending what she went through growing up during the second world war in London. At the age of seven, she had to do all the family grocery shopping because her mother was never home.

She grew up with one older sister and no father. Her mother was a horrible, wicked woman, and the first time I ever saw my mother cry was when we went to visit my grandmother. With six suitcases, my sister five and I seven arrived at my grandmother's home in England in the pouring rain. My grandmother opened the door, told my mother we were early, and we had to go away into the village and find somewhere to sit for a couple of hours, but we could leave our suitcases with her. My mother started to cry.

My mother trained as an RN and worked in one of the large London hospitals. She met my father on vacation to the Isle of Wight while staying at my Nana's B&B. My father was back home on the Isle of Wight, visiting his family as he was living in Victoria, B.C. at the time. My Nana encouraged him to take my mom and her girlfriend out on a picnic one day, but I do not think he minded too much. My mother kept in touch with my father, and one spring day, she came out to Canada for a holiday and never went back! All I know is that she phoned her mother and asked her to collect her items in London and keep them for her to go through the next time she visited.

My mother tried to give us what we needed and did her best. I am sure I was not the easiest child as I hated to be hugged and touched. I preferred to be on my own and play quietly, and I wasn't as social as my sister, who was a bubbly, outgoing child. My mother and I were like oil and water. She and I didn't get along very well, and I became independent at an early age. My mother had many horrible experiences with my grandmother that she needed to work through, but unfortunately, she never dealt with it, so it was passed down to my sister and me. Our cheerful home could become dark very quickly.

We were never abused physically, but emotionally, watch out. If my mother wanted to get us to do something, she used scare tactics. If she wanted me to obey her without a fight, she would tell me something horrific. For example, she feared big dogs. If she saw a dog tied up at the grocery store or outside the shops, she would say to my little sister and me, "If you touch that dog, he will bite you," or when I wanted to go with my friends to a mall across the river in another city, she would say, "If you drive across that bridge, you will have an accident." What brought the most terror into my heart was when she was having a bad day, she would say to us, "If you don't do what I say, I will put my head in the gas oven and turn it on." That brought absolute fear into my sister and me. She used this threat until I was old enough to hand her the book of matches and offered to light one for her!

Life looked all sparkly and shiny on the outside, but once you walked through the door, there could be bouts of terror and sadness. When life was fun, which was most of the time, it was amazing. I don't want to give the impression that my whole childhood was awful because that is not the case. We had many happy memories that I still think about today. I know my mom had demons, but she rarely drank and never physically abused us. I believe that if she had been allowed to get professional help, she would have been much happier.

As I grew up, the tension between my mother and I grew too. I loved her but no longer wanted to live with her. I went to UBC right out of high school. I was taking education courses, and I was enjoying going to university, but I was finding it difficult living at home and attending school. I needed to get a job other than my summer childcare and I pondered what to do. I did get a job at an alarm monitoring station in East Vancouver, and I worked the graveyard shift. The money was good for a student, and I enjoyed the quiet nights and being able to have an income.

The year of my sister's graduation, I took driving lessons and became a little more independent. The summer of my new job, my sister graduated high school, and my mother and my sister took a trip to England and Europe to visit family and some friends. I stayed home with my dad to take care of the house while he was working. I enjoyed my newfound independence when they were gone, as I took care of the household responsibilities. It was so nice to be free of tension and constant mother/daughter bickering.

An opportunity to move out arose in the basement of a family I babysat for. I moved out into their one-room basement suite with a miniature sink and stove in the room and a shared shower and toilet. I scrubbed and scrubbed the shower and washroom, painted my room a bright white, and put up pretty, patterned curtains to make it seem very homey. I remember feeling so grown up and independent. I started to make some pretty important decisions that may not have been wise at the time, but sometimes pride gets in the way of letting you see what all the consequences will be once you make that decision.

I remember when my mother came home, and I told her I had moved out. Her reaction was priceless. She smiled and said, "good." Then she thought about it for a second or two and added, "as long as you are safe and happy." I knew it was the right decision as we both would enjoy each other's company much better with me not living under her roof.

Once I got a taste for my independence, I decided not to return to university in the fall. I know now that making that decision would alter the course of my life, but at that moment, I believed that was the right one for me. I never did return to university, but in later years, I did take some correspondence courses and enjoyed them and did very well. If you are wondering, I had three courses to finish to get my teacher's degree, but I never did finish. I wish I had finished, but sometimes we cannot change a decision.

In 2000, I thought I had found the perfect life partner. It seemed great, and I fell hard for him. He had some baggage, but it was nothing I couldn't fix! Or so I thought. I married him, and we started our life together. Unfortunately, I didn't get any of the things that I genuinely wanted out of the relationship. No children, no stability. I was traveling down a rabbit hole, deeper and deeper, and I saw no way out.

I remember lying in bed one night, and I kept thinking about all the decisions I had made, and where I had ended up, all I wanted to do was die. I asked God to let me die because I was so unhappy and did not know how to get out of the situation. I wanted the sadness and depression to end, but I was so scared to get out. I believed that love could fix anything, but the problem was that I no longer believed in love, only sadness, and I had turned into a person that I no longer liked, so how could anyone else like me. I had very few friends, and I do not blame anyone for not wanting to be around me as I did not even want to be around myself. I needed to change my situation, but I didn't know how, nor did I have the inner strength to do it.

I wanted to start again, in a parallel world where none of the anger, hatred, or hurt had ever happened. I wanted to reverse my decision for moving out of my parent's house that summer and have a do-over. I wanted to be a teacher and start a new path with a different outcome. I wanted to be happy and go on holidays with friends and family. I wanted a family of my own.

Sometimes you do not get to make the decisions that alter your life course, sometimes they are thrust at you like a brick coming through a window at full speed, and you either move or get hit. I got hit full on and with a new level of pain and hurt that I did not know existed. I was forced to make a decision that I did not want to make or ever thought I would have to make. I decided to separate from my husband in 2014. It was hard at first. I was lost, like someone in the woods at night. I could not find a way out. The toll of the unhappy years had affected me so deeply that I was laid off from the job that I genuinely loved. I understand why it happened, but it still stung. I was lost in my marriage and now in my career.

I decided to take time to take care of myself. For the next year, I worked on myself. I climbed back out of that rabbit hole and up onto the anthill next to it. I was getting back to feeling like me. I took the time to love me again.

Despite all of my personal growth, things still didn't get better. The rental house I lived in sold, and I had to find a new place to live. I still wasn't officially divorced, and we were still in contact with each other. Part of my personal growth and healing was to make amends with my past demons and forgive. I was having a hard time finding a place to live within my budget, and it just so happened that my ex was also being evicted.

So, I made another decision that I should have thought harder about. I decided to move back in with my ex but within very specific parameters. We had separate bedrooms, and we split the cost of everything evenly. Even with these established rules, the debts mounted, and the situation reverted to what it was before. This time, though, something was different. I felt different and much stronger. I started to make new plans for myself.

In the meantime, my father had retired, and my parents moved to a beautiful gulf island. They were happy, or so I thought. My sister and I learned that mom's memory was fading, she was changing, and dad could not cope. He was doing most of the cooking and fully in charge of their lives. In 2018, my sister and I went to visit them at every opportunity we could. I spent more time with my parents that year than I had in twenty years.

I saw how mom was declining, but she wasn't bad enough yet to live in long-term care. I decided to resign from my job and move to the island to help my father take care of my mother. I needed to be free of all responsibilities or ties before I left, which meant I needed my divorce to become official. I started the divorce process in the fall of 2018 and picked December 16, 2018, as the date I was going to make the big move to the island.

During the final months of working and living in the lower main-land, I experienced many emotions. I was very conflicted about moving to a small island and leaving my friends behind. The decision to move was not easy, and I took the time required before I made my final decision. It was ironic that I had spent the first part of my life trying to get away from my mother, and now, in the latter part of my life, I was being asked to come back to help take care of her.

The move happened, the divorce happened, and I was now living on the island helping my father with my mother's care. It took a long time to get into a routine. There were doctor's appointments and assessments, and I had to assimilate into a new way of life. I didn't know anyone except a few of my parent's friends who I had met over the years, so I needed to make some friends of my own. It did not take long for the new friends to appear, and I realized that I was not shy after all and I could make friends easily, and I was a nice person to be around. I joined mom's church, and I became involved in the Prayer Shawl group and started to crochet again. I had done it in my younger years but never had the time to start again until now.

I joined the Elementary School Hot Lunch Program through an amazing organization on the island called PHC (People for a Healthy Community) and met many people through that and had a wonderful time creating some delicious lunches for the elementary school children. I was asked to help at the Annual Summer BBQ and put on a fundraiser through the community hall. While I was serving the side dishes, I tried to talk to as many people as possible and had an amazing time. I was then asked if I would be interested in sitting as a board member, to which I said yes. I am now in my second term as a board member for the community hall.

Life was going great, and mom was enjoying all the new activities we were doing together. Then COVID-19 hit, and we stopped dead in our tracks. All of the programs were canceled. No church, no seniors' programs, no going out for coffee or lunches in town or on the island. Life became very restricted. We continue to make it work, and mom is still as happy as ever. I am still busy on skype and doing some of the things that kept me busy before.

In the summer of 2020, I started feeling unwell. After consulting a few doctors, I had an ultrasound, an MRI, and a CT Scan, as well as a couple of complete examinations. It was so scary, to say the least. Then I got the call. It was stage four cancer. There was a tumor in my uterus and my cervix, and the cancer had spread to my lungs and liver. I was shocked, and the only person I wanted to talk to was my sister. I called her, and the first thing I said to her was, "I don't want to DIE."

How ironic that all I wanted to do was die all those years ago, and now I was in for the fight of my life to stay alive. I didn't want to say goodbye yet. I became extremely ill in September and ended up in the hospital for a week, and started my chemo treatments in October. I have had six treatments so far. I've lost my hair, energy, volunteer work, and outings, but I am still alive, and I thank God every day. When I open my eyes in the morning, I say to myself, "Everyone dies, but today is not my day." I live each day happy to be alive.

I have a CT Scan on Friday, February 5, 2021, and it will determine the next steps. The oncologists have told me that it is not curable, but I will be doing everything I can to knock it back down and give me more years to keep living.

I still crochet shawls for the church, but not as fast or frequently as I used to. I have a new routine with mom, and she is healthy and happy. Life is noticeably quiet, and we do not see many people other than the ones in our bubble, but that will change eventually, too, and we can get back to our outside adventures.

This life-changing health event has made me readjust my priorities, and I realized that I need to do more things that take me out of my comfort zone. I created a bucket list and at the top of the list is to travel to Tahiti and Bora Bora with my sister and some of our friends. I plan on doing this for my 60<sup>th</sup> birthday in two years.

As I reflect on my life and take stock of what I have learned, I realize how much I have changed. I want to live and make every day count. The times where I wanted to die have long since passed, and I am glad I am still here to fight.

It took a life-altering event to make me realize that what I want is the same thing as what I need and that I will not waste time dwelling on what was awful, but instead, I want to create joy, no matter how hard the road is to get there.

**Vanessa Downer**

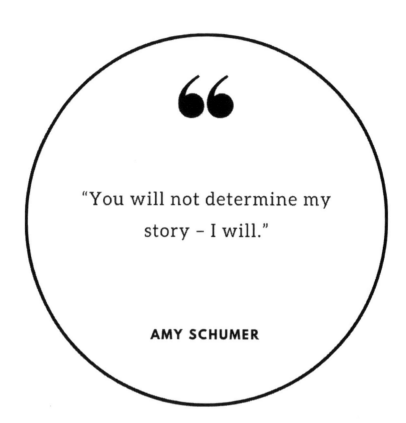

"You will not determine my
story – I will."

**AMY SCHUMER**

# TWO

## Tales From an Expert Former Hider

### HOW I KICKED THE HIDING HABIT AND LEARNED HOW TO SPEAK UP

It's the middle of the night. I'm lying in a bunk bed, wide awake, listening to the soft sounds of my kids breathing. There's no fresh air in the room, and my brain is like a grasshopper on speed. *How the hell did we end up in a women's shelter? What will happen if he finds us?* My kids slept on while my mind jittered. I asked myself those same questions over and over until I was too exhausted and fell asleep. Five days earlier, I was working as a program manager for an international bank in Amsterdam. Now I jumped out of my skin at every unexpected sound.

I fled my home with my two kids, ages two and four, with only a backpack, a carrier bag with clothes, a doll, and a child's potty. My kids and I were completely traumatized from a sudden outburst of domestic violence, which could have killed us. I'd told him I was leaving him, and he had flipped out of control.

Here I was, at a shelter, lying in a grey metal bed, on a sweaty, plastic-covered mattress, unable to stop thinking or get any rest. I remember how one time, a social worker asked me to count cheese slices in the fridge to see if there were enough for lunch, which seemed simple enough. First, I kept losing track of the count. Then I couldn't remember the total. I tried four or five times, but in the end, I had to say I couldn't do it. My brain was so jumpy; it couldn't even focus enough to count to ten. The week before, I'd been running an IT program with a $22 million budget. And now I couldn't even count cheese slices. I felt humiliated, useless, and ashamed. It was a dark time. I was either hiding in our stuffy room with the curtains closed day and night or walking endlessly at top speed. I was terrified of being found, and I couldn't sit still. My body needed to keep moving. It took me a year to be able to sleep through the night again.

Over the course of those twelve months, I learned how to cover my tracks so we couldn't be found. I became an expert at hiding. I learned that I could have my bank statements sent to a post box instead of my home address and that I wasn't traceable on my computer if I was reading an email. I avoided photos which might end up on social media. I learned never to tell anyone where I was.

In the process of hiding my physical location, I also became an expert at hiding my emotions. At the shelter, the social workers had all the power. If they felt you weren't doing your best, they could postpone when you could move to your new home. My friends were too scared to help me, and my family was in the UK. I had nowhere to go, so I learned to 'behave.' I did what I needed to do to get us out of the shelter as quickly as I could. I was polite and followed the rules, even if on the inside I was raging at the indignity of my situation. Imagine being a responsible, well-educated woman with a respectable career, being told, "Your child can go to school A or school B. They are the only schools we work with." My life had been uprooted and ripped apart and the shelter itself gave me an intense, powerless feeling that I felt forced to hide. My feelings went underground so that we could get away from there.

Over the course of that year, we moved seven times. Three times within the shelter, one halfway house, two different apartments, and then finally our own home. I bought the kids posters and glued them to cardboard and covered them with plastic so they'd keep. My son chose an Elvis poster, and my daughter chose one with some cute babies in flowers on it. We took those posters to every home and hung them next to their beds to help them feel at home. I took the kids to our new house before our move, so they could get used to the idea. The living room was filled with moving boxes, so I used one for them to sit on and used another as a table. They sat there surrounded by a wall of boxes eating Happy Meals, smiling. All I saw were piles of unpacked boxes, but they saw an amazing place to play. I knew that it was all going to be okay.

My lowest moment came on a stormy February day. I had to walk my son to school with my daughter in the buggy and then walk back home again. In the morning, the wind was blowing hard, and the trees were waving furiously. I collected him for lunch, and the path was full of puddles, and the wind was gusting. I had to hold onto the buggy for dear life. We got home and changed into dry clothes. I walked him back to school, and we had to step over branches that had fallen off the trees in the wind. When I went to collect him at the end of the day, I felt like I was coming down with the flu. The rain was heavy and relentless. I could feel massive, cold drops running down my back into my underwear, making me shiver. My son looked at me and said, "Look, Mamma!" I looked up through the drops of water falling off my hood and saw him pointing at a puddle. The rain was pounding down, and enormous drops were smacking onto the surface of the puddle and splashing back up. "Silver!" he said. When the drops splashed back up, they looked like silver. Right there, in that instant, I realized that I'd been so focused on getting us home that I'd missed the silver. "Yes," I said, "isn't it beautiful?"

The kids kept me going in so many ways. I remember one after-noon, just after I had been fired from my job in Amsterdam, that I longed to get into bed, pull the blankets over me and just sleep. One voice inside me, said "Lynn, give yourself a break, you want to sleep. You've been through enough," and another voice said, "Don't go to sleep, it will take you weeks to get up again. Don't give into this." I couldn't decide which voice to listen to. They kept their discussion up long enough that in the end, I had to go and collect my son from school. Without the kids, I would have climbed into that bed and disappeared under a deep, dark blanket of depression.

When you go through something traumatic, your personality gets stripped back to the essence of who you are. Through my experiences, I found out that I always find humor in any situation. I'm so grateful for this. While I was at the shelter, I also learned to take things one step at a time, and that routines helped me get more done. I'd lost my job in Amsterdam, and I had nowhere else I could go because all my family was in the UK. There were no international banks where I was living, so there was no logical place for me to work. I had to rethink everything. *What was I going to do? Was this the moment to finally start my own business?* I'd wanted to for years but never knew what I could sell, and I feared the risk. In the end, I figured if I survived everything I'd already been through, what's the worst thing that could happen? So, I started my business.

For the first few years, I really struggled. I didn't want to say where I lived or what my phone number was; selling my services felt uncomfortable. I kept plugging away at the business, but I was making progress at a snail's pace, and I still felt way outside my comfort zone. I have this strategy that I use called the mirror test. If I look at myself in the mirror, I ask myself, do I feel good about what I see? It's not about makeup or hair, it's about the sparkle in my eyes. Do I really look alive? Do I look happy? Do I really feel like me? Can I see the 5-year-old Lynn in there, trusting and excited about all the adventures that my life is going to bring me? I looked in the mirror, and I didn't like what I saw. I looked timid, angry, and distrustful. I realized that if this went on, I would become bitter and the sort of person people avoid. I really didn't want that.

I wanted to change, but I didn't know how. How could I just stop thinking about my trauma when it had become automatic? How could I stop being so afraid? Was my fear justified or had it become a habit? Thankfully, the universe had a way of answering my questions. I found that if I asked a question clearly and was ready to hear the answer, an answer always came. And often surprisingly fast. Some of the answers I found were meditation, *The Work* by Byron Katie, and Emotional Freedom Techniques. I started to grow as a person, to let my walls down, to tap into my softness, and to see what I had learned from the horrors I'd been through. What happened to me in my marriage wasn't my fault. Domestic violence or the threat of violence is never justified. But it was a learning experience that made me tougher and made me rethink my values.

As I learned and grew in my personal development, I learned and grew in my business too. Eventually, I was able to stop hiding and to make myself visible. Step by step I started giving presentations, joining online meetings, going live online, and speaking my mind. It took an enormous amount of courage each time I took a new step. I was no longer afraid my ex would find me, but from time to time I would still be triggered by something that sent me right back into hiding again. Then it could take weeks for me to come back out of my shell.

While I was doing my own work, I started to notice something. It turned out I wasn't the only one in hiding. I also wasn't the only entrepreneur in hiding. And I certainly wasn't the only woman. I met so many talented, friendly people who were hiding, and I became curious.

Over the years, I've heard many stories about hiding. Stories about tyrannical teachers and parents, being bullied by classmates, of not being noticed, of losing self-confidence because of dyslexia or ADHD, stories of feeling like an outsider, dealing with racism and homophobia, and stories that sounded a lot like mine. I noticed something else from the stories that I heard from women. A common theme that emerged from the stories was how women have been brought up to adapt to others and to be nice. Women learn to say, "Sorry to bother you" and "What do you think?" They are taught to hide their thoughts and feelings, and they learn to adapt to others. What I know now is that the world needs our warmth, talents, and experiences. It needs women to stop hiding. It's time for us to step up and start making things better. Women, and especially women entrepreneurs, need to be out there solving problems, helping people, and making the world a better place. We need to speak our thoughts and feelings, no matter what anyone else thinks. And we really need to stop hiding.

Today, through my own business, I'm helping online coaches, trainers, and healers speak up, so the world can listen. I'm helping them find their voice to express who they really are and what they really do so they can go out and help others grow. I listen with my heart, so I can feel what they are saying and to what they're not saying. Often what someone isn't saying tells me most of all. When I've listened, I can help them find the words they need. They feel seen and heard, and that gives them the loving space they need to grow in confidence, and they feel more able to do what they were born to do.

I've learned that we women hide too much and too often, and I'm on a mission to help us to stop hiding and instead to start shining. The world today and the future world my children will live in needs to hear from women who speak up.

Are you with me?

**Lynn Coleman**

"It's funny how, when things seem the darkest, moments of beauty present themselves in the most unexpected places."

**KAREN MARIE MONING**

THREE

# The Cabin in the Woods

A YOUNG GIRL'S STORY OF SURVIVAL IN THE
WILDERNESS

In May of 1969, I had just turned eleven, and my brother Richard was thirteen. My parents took us out of school early that year so we could make the move from Toronto, Ontario, to a small town in Northern Ontario called Ahmic Harbour. Neither my mom nor stepdad knew how to drive, and to this day, I can't remember how we got there.

When we arrived, we had to fight our way through thick bush, and we got tangled and scratched up by thorn bushes. We needed to reach higher ground so we could find a place to make camp, my parents said. I remember the foul smell of rotten eggs. My mother told me it was the odor coming from the nearby swamp. There was bush for as far as the eye could see and beyond. We'd never been camping in our lives. In fact, we had never left the city. My parents finally told my brother and I that we had moved here so we could build a cabin and have our own home. I remember thinking how the hell were we going to build a cabin?

When we reached higher ground, some distance from the swamp, my parents decided to set up camp. We started to clear the land and set up makeshift tents. The mosquitoes were horrible. Jim, my stepdad, lit a fire and burned dry pine boughs, which created a lot of smoke to help clear away the mosquitoes. That was the first night of many long nights to come where my brother and I would take turns swishing the blankets back and forth to keep the mosquitoes off the other while we slept.

Over the next few days, we made the camp a little cosier. We cut fresh pine boughs to place under our sleeping bags. I was grateful that I couldn't smell the swamp from where we were. The warm brown earth felt nice on my bare feet. I never wore shoes again unless we had to go into town.

We decided we had to cut a trail from our camp down to the road. We had some basic tools like an old rusty buck saw and some bush loppers. We also marked the trees so we could find our way back to camp. All of us ventured out to try and find water, and on our journey, we realized there was a lot of swamp land around us. I could taste the stagnant air and hear the slurp of the mud and the frogs croaking. We found a lake a couple miles down the road, and from that day on, Richard and I had to travel to that lake almost every day to get water. The town dump was near the lake, and we scavenged for things we could use in camp. There was a shell of an old washing machine that worked great as a stove top over the fire pit. We later found lots of handy items. My parents didn't bring much with them, just a few tools and essentials.

My mother, stepdad and brother began to cut down trees and skin them. I helped carry the logs. It took a couple of months to get the foundation finished and logs cut and peeled for the walls; after that, Jim left.

My stepfather was an unusual fellow. I knew nothing about him, if memory serves me right, he and my mother got married three years ago but I had no idea who he was. The only thing I knew about him was that he drank a lot and was a camp cook. Looking back, I think we moved to the bush so they could get away from the temptations of the city. I remember coming home from school one day in the early afternoon when we lived in Toronto, and there were cop cars and ambulances on my street. I ran to see what was happening and to my embarrassment, saw that my stepfather had passed out drunk on the neighbor's lawn. I wondered if any of the kids in my class knew who he was.

Kids at school already had enough reasons to pick on me. I was a scrawny little kid with tattered clothes and often had holes in my shoes. If anyone picked on me too often, I would punch their lights out, and they would never pick on me again. My brother never seemed to have that problem. All the girls loved him, and many befriended me just to get to know him. He was so good looking, or so the girls would tell me.

Jim never returned after the foundation was built and we never saw him again. We were left to finish the cabin ourselves. It was late summer now, the days were long, and we worked hard. The only time we were free was on Sunday afternoons after we filled up the old water tank that we got from the dump. It would take Richard and I three trips to the lake and back and all morning to fill the tank up. Later, we started to take the wash tub instead of pails. We could carry a lot more water that way and got done a lot faster, which gave us more time to spend in town. My brother held one side of the tub and me the other, and I remember it being so heavy and it was so hot out the sweat would cling to the back of my shirt. I would envision how great it was going to be to jump into the cool clean harbor lake after we were finished.

The town of Ahmic Harbour, we figured, was about three miles away from camp, and in the opposite direction of the lake. Ahmic Harbour was a quaint little town with one small grocery store and the Ahmic Harbor Inn. The population at the time was about a hundred people. As far as we could tell, only one family had kids, and they had like 15 of them. We would get together with them and head down to the harbor for a swim. Ahmic lake was crystal clear and cool. We had to watch out for the huge dragonflies that would dive bomb us. Also, we had to make sure we checked ourselves all over for leeches when we got out. I had the blood suckers all over my back one time and my brother pulled them off me. It hurt like hell. They have teeth and they bite you. Afterward, we would go to the little grocery store and pick up some supplies. My parents had a credit set up with the store.

We all developed a daily routine. While my mom and brother felled trees, I often went to pick berries. As I walked through the bush towards the road one day to go berry picking, I came across this very large tree that had been cut down or fallen, as I got closer, I saw my brother's legs sticking out from under the tree. I ran, my heart pounding. I was panic stricken, shouting at the top of my lungs RICHARD RICHARD I had no idea what I would do when I got there. I certainly couldn't lift the tree, but I ran to him anyways. As I got closer, I could see there was a bit of a gully under the tree, and then I saw my brother's face, the funny guy that he is, trying his best not to laugh. I could have killed him. He was always pranking me or trying to scare me.

One day after I had been picking berries for a few hours, I heard a noise. I looked up and less than three feet away stood a huge black bear. I threw my basket of berries in the air. I ran like the wind, thorns ripping at my arms. I tripped on tangled roots, but I dared not look behind me in case he was chasing me. I found my brother and knew we had to go back and get my basket of berries. My brother only came because he wanted to see the bear.

When we got there, we found the basket, but the berries were gone. We had to pick quickly, or my mom would be angry that I wasn't doing my chores, or she'd accuse me of eating all the berries myself, or that I was making up stories, and she would take the switch to my bare little legs. The switch was a flexible thin stick that felt like a whip, and it stung worse than any belt.

I did most of the chores around camp, and I got pretty good at chopping wood and making fires. My brother was the only one who could get the fire going in the rain, though. My dishwashing pit was set up in front of two giant pine trees. I felt a sense of awe and comfort when I looked at these trees. They felt like friends who never judged me. I'd watch the birds flit in and out of the branches and see the squirrels constantly running up and down the tree trunks chattering away. I would talk to them and I was sure they could hear me and feel my very soul. I wondered how far their roots traveled and if they connected with the roots of other trees. I also wondered if they felt it when one of their own kind was fallen. Did they look at the log cabin as a graveyard of naked trees? This place was starting to grow on me, and the solitude soothed me.

On the way home one night after being out on the lake fishing, the sky was black, there was no moon to be seen. As we came up the hill to our camp, we saw thousands of eyes in the trees. When we reached our camp, it was completely destroyed. Whatever food we had was gone. Raccoons were everywhere. Over the next few days, there were many of them around, and my mother decided she would have to shoot one of the older ones in the hopes that it would scare the others away. She got out her 22 and shot one. It was a pretty good shot, and it died instantly. The raccoons never returned. She said she was going to skin it so we could eat it but then decided it was too old and the meat would be tough.

My mother was small framed and stood about 5'2" with thick long black hair. She always wore her hair in two braids. During the time we lived there, my mother always wore gumboots, and she told us she wasn't afraid of anything except snakes. She loved being out in the woods. She said, "I would rather run into a bear any day than run into a man on a dark street in the city."

One morning, I heard my mother scream. I looked up and she was over in the little vegetable garden where nothing ever grew. She stood, frozen. I grabbed the ax leaning against the woodpile. I ran as fast as my shaky legs would carry me. Where was my damn brother when we needed him? I could see my mother as she forced a smile, but nothing could disguise the rising panic in her eyes. Twigs snapped beneath my feet. I tried to slow my pace and not make a sound. There, about a foot away from my mother, it laid as motionless as her. As I neared, I saw the rattle. Terror seized me. I heard my mother's shrill scream, "Kill it! Kill it!" I swung the ax with all my might and hit the ground. I swung again and missed. I looked at its triangular head with a greyish brown body and catlike eyes. It wasn't very big, maybe two feet, but I knew it was poisonous. The snake darted toward me and hissed. I heard the buzz of its tail when it shook its rattle. I swung again, but the ax flew out of my hands. The rattlesnake was close enough to strike my shoeless feet. It didn't move. Maybe it's scared, I thought. My brother suddenly appeared from nowhere, grabbed the ax, and before I could close my eyes, I witnessed the cold blade strike the snake. It was all over. My mother later told me the snake was a massasauga rattler, which she said could make you seriously ill but not kill you. I wondered how far the nearest hospital was.

Our closest neighbor lived about a mile down the road in a real house. They had two boys. Ted, the younger one was a year older than me, he was a nerdy little guy, skinny as hell, he would come over and hang out a bit. Ted told us his mom thought our mom was crazy. She would say stuff like, "She's crazy living up there in the bush with no running water, not even a toilet. And trying to build a cabin with two kids, what will they do come winter? They will freeze to death."

He also said he knew how to use a witching stick and that he could find water with it. We had told Ted we had to walk to Love lake every day to get water. He said he would use a witching stick to find water on our land. I didn't even know if it was our land or if we just rented it. The parents didn't tell us much. Ted cut a forked branch from a live tree and showed us how it's done. "Grab both ends of Y with your palms facing upwards and hold it horizontally so that it points in front of you. Keep your hands loose and slowly walk around, and as you, near water, the rod will bend toward the ground then you have to hold the rod tight, or it will fly out of your hands." He would walk around with the witching stick. As luck would have it, he found a spot. We saw the stick bend toward the ground and shake. Richard and I dug every evening. We had to use a hammer and a chisel because it was mostly rock. It took a long time, but we stayed at it every day, and sure enough, we hit water. I remember the water was crystal clear. Now the only time we had to go to the lake was to catch fish.

Richard and I went fishing one evening and the black flies were so thick that we had to wear panty hose over our heads to keep them from getting into our eyes and mouth. We were determined to catch something before we left otherwise, there would be no dinner again.

About a month after Jim left, the man at the grocery store told us the grocery bill had not been paid in a while and cut off our store credit. Ever since we were living on fish and berries. Our fishing gear consisted of a pole and a wire with a hook. Back then, you could use live bait, so we used some worms and when we ran out, we would use other parts of the fish we caught like the eyes, they made good bait. That night we didn't catch anything, and we had to get back to camp. It was already dark out, and we didn't have flash-lights, only the light of the moon. Richard used to tell me scary stories on our walks back to camp, like how something was going to get me and kill me, and I would be a corpse left in the bush. He always tried to scare me.

That night, on our way back, we sensed something was behind us. We turned around and could see shadowy outlines and fiery white eyes. Holy shit it was a pack of wolves. I started to run but my brother said no. "He said to try and find some sticks." We scurried around and quickly picked up some sticks and walked backward. They just kept following us. We were fucking terrified. My brother started throwing sticks at them, and we kept picking up more and throwing them until they finally backed off. I had never been so scared in my life. Then we saw a light up ahead and it was my mother with the lantern. She was waiting for us at the bush entrance. I don't think we'd have found our way through the bush without it.

Times were getting desperate for food, so the next day my mother and brother went out fishing. I sat by the fire and looked up at the sky. It was lit with grey, and the sun was just dipping down through the darker clouds. The trees felt the last warmth of the sun as the night moved in. It was getting late, and I was getting scared sitting by myself, especially after the terrifying wolf encounter. I added more logs to the crackling fire and moved closer. I was so hoping they would catch some fish. It got dark quickly. The light cast by the flames moved across the dark trunks of the trees, twisting and curling into ghostly shapes, scaring me half to death. The fear took my mind off the gnawing hunger pains in my stomach. Finally, I saw the lantern bobbing up and down as my mom and brother approached. I could smell the faint odor of fresh fish.

It was mid-October now, and the exterior of the log cabin was almost finished, But It still needed a roof. The roof was a big job and I didn't know if my mom knew how to build it. She and Richard were out peeling the pine trees they had just chopped down and I was alone in camp when suddenly, I heard a man's voice screaming. "Help! Help!" I thought, what the heck, who could that be up here? I decided I better go find out. The bush was thick if you didn't know where you were going.

When I found the man, he was sitting on the ground, breathless with small cuts on his hands and arms. He was wearing dress clothes, and his shirt was torn. He gave me a strange look. I couldn't remember the last time I combed my hair; my feet and lower legs were completely red from mosquito bites. I must have looked like some kind of wild child. He said, "Thank god, I've been wandering for hours lost in this dreaded bush trying to find your place."

He was a small man and not much bigger than my brother. He looked distraught. I asked him why he was looking for our place? He said, "I need to talk to your mother. Can you please take me to her?" As we walked, I wondered so many things. Is he a relative I never met? Why would he come all the way out here? He said his name was Brian and he was here to help us. When we got to our camp, he looked surprised to see the log cabin. Richard and my mom showed up carrying another log. They were startled to see a stranger in our camp. I introduced them and told them that he was here to help us.

Brian told us he was from the Children's Aid Society, and he had come to take us away from here. He said we were supposed to be in school and that we would never survive the winter here. He told us that in the winter, it gets as cold -25 to -30 degrees Celsius and that we would freeze to death. I tried to argue with him and tell him we had plenty of wood to keep us warm and that we learned more here than we ever would in school. I was so angry I was shaking. I could feel my face getting red with the sting of tears. We had worked so hard and had come so far. I ran from them all into the bush. The tears flowed. I didn't want to go back to the city. I hated the city.

After a while, Richard found me and said, "Come on, kid, we have to go with the man." My brother said it was probably Ted's mom who had called these people. I thought we were all going together, but only Richard and I went. Brian said we would be able to see our mother again when she got things in order. Like when she finds a job and a decent place to live.

Twenty years later, when my mother died, my brother and I returned to the cabin to scatter her ashes. We knew it was the only place she was ever happy. Nothing had changed. It was still all bush and swamp land. We found the entrance right away even though it was all grown in and there were no markings left on the trees to find our way. The log cabin stood just as we had left it. Only it looked smaller than how I remembered it.

Your past can be empowering if you embrace it and accept that you can't change it. After the acceptance is when the healing begins. This is the start of letting go and moving on to become the beautiful soul you are.

*"Lotus flowers lead harrowing journeys. Their seeds sprout in murky swamp water, thick with dirt and debris and snarls of roots. For a lotus to bloom, she must forge her way through this terrible darkness, avoid being eaten by fish and insects, and keep pressing onward, innately knowing, or at least hoping, that there is sunlight somewhere above the water's surface, if she can only summon the strength to get there. And when she does, she emerges unscathed by her journey and blooms triumphantly." – Sarah Jio*

**Marisa Lavallee**

"If the only prayer you ever say in your entire life is 'Thank You' it will be enough."

**MEISTER ECKHART**

# FOUR

## Day Zero

### THE DAY THAT CHANGED MY LIFE APRIL 10, 1987

They call the first day of a baby being born day zero. Which I think is odd.

In my mind, it was Adam's first day as a living, breathing human and my first day as a twenty-three-year-old mother who never had a maternal bone in her body.

A day I will never forget, not only because of these two significant things but also because of how my day was turned upside down by one single doctor and I do not even remember his name. His words and lack of bedside manner as he spoke to me explaining the facts:

"Good afternoon Mrs. Beck: I am Adam's pediatrician. He is over at Children's Hospital right now, having more tests run, but at this point, we know that he has something called Tetralogy of Fallot (better known as Blue Babies syndrome). He will have open and closed heart surgeries by the time he is five, and his life expectancy is ........." And he lost me there.

I remember this pivotal day like it was yesterday, and it shaped many of my choices for years to come.

I was a young mom and the maternal instinct kicked in for me ten months earlier. I never had that urge that many women get. I was too busy skiing or being out in the wilderness and enjoying life to be bothered with the thought of getting married and having children. Yet here I was, and I had a sick one to boot.

I had met Dan (Adam's dad) in Mexico on a fun trip with a company called Bust Loose Holidays based out of Calgary, Alberta. A company that focused on taking university students after exams on affordable, fun trips. Mexico, after final exams or Jackson Hole after Christmas exams and house boating on the Shuswap mid-summer. I had followed Dan out to Vancouver. Stars in my eyes, believing all that was wonderful was happening to me. Princess marries the Dentist (that was a book title one of my girlfriends had sent over to me at that time). Dan had just graduated from Dentistry at the ripe age of 21, and his friend had bought a practice in Vancouver, British Columbia, and wanted Dan to run it. I left Calgary to go for the weekend and never came home. We were married the following year, back down in Mexico, as I was now working for the company, so it just seemed to make sense to do it there, where we met, with a whole bunch of friends and some family, not have the expense of a large wedding, so we eloped in May of 1986.

Adam showed up the following April, much to our surprise as I was told I had endometriosis and I probably could not have children, but the best thing I could do for my body was to get pregnant. Jordan, his brother, arrived on November 11, 1989.

When I reflect on that time of youthful hope and idealism, I wish I understood how difficult life could be. I had lived a charmed life, relatively speaking, never saw my parents fight, family holidays, big brother taking care of me, never really wanting for much, and the freedom to do pretty much as I wanted. I was a trusted, good girl.

Dan and I did not make it, sick child, no relationship skills, our youth, inexperience, and the bank giving us way too much money. It was just too much for a young couple to endure. However, we have remained friends, neighbors (the boys could walk to and from our homes), and he is Bill's (my husband since 2001) and my dentist to this day. I am proud of how we have co-parented and made the best of an exceedingly difficult time in our lives.

Six weeks after Adam was born, I went for our first check-up with his pediatrician back into the city. All I remember was the doctor. asking me if I drove and if I knew the quickest route to Children's Hospital. If I did not, he would call an ambulance. I was like a deer in headlights as I heard him on the phone explaining to whomever was on the other end of the call that the patient's name was Beck, Timothy Adam, and he would be there STAT. Off I went with no clue what was going on and what was going to unfold.

The realization that his closed heart surgery (a Blalock shunt was being put in) was immediate, forget him being two years old like we were told, so his heart could grow a little bit more to make it easier for the surgeons to operate. Again, as a mother, my experience or lack thereof was not knowing the difference between a blue baby and a pink baby. Silly me.

I will never forget barging through the ICU doors knowing that he was out of surgery and doing ok. I became panic-stricken as I looked for the board that had his name on it and what bed he was in. I was terrified of not knowing what to expect in the upcoming moments.

I arrived at his bedside; I was just a little too soon. The nurses were doing their final prep, putting the tube in his nose or down his throat. I cannot quite remember. However, what I do remember, as I was stopped in my tracks, was his color. He was pink, a little pink ball of joy. He was still asleep, but I will never forget the wonder and awe I felt as I looked down and marveled at just how beautiful he was and how fortunate I was to live in a time and a place where procedures like this could be done.

Two and a half years later, Jordan arrived. Planned, expected, and monitored he was. I was traveling monthly for check-ups during my pregnancy to BCCH (British Columbia Children's Hospital) as they were tracking his progress. Adams Tetralogy is noted as a congenital heart defect, unknown as to why it happens, yet it occurs in the uterine. Hence the continued monitoring with the possibility of being able to learn something if Jordan ended up with the same defect. I was hooked up to machines with a gallery of cardiologists, doctors, nurses and tech people. You name it, it was my monthly routine.

Jordan's day was upon us and me being the personality that I am (highest and best use, quickest way through), I thought, let's book Adam's check up the same time I was scheduled for my c-section delivery of his little brother. One trip into the city to the facility where both appointments could be done, kill two birds with one stone, good idea, right? Think again, the news from the doctor was not expected. We were like a deer in headlights. Here we go again. His major correction (open heart) has to be done ASAP, we were told.

That following week, back we were at BCCH, with a newborn and my mother to keep us company and help in any way a mother could help a daughter going through was I was going through. My mom was an angel that was sent to help me. I have no clue how I would have gotten through any of this without her. Thank you again, mom. I am ever grateful.

As we forged ahead towards the unknown with the fear of the possible outcome that no one wanted to talk about, I learned to appreciate this facility, these nurses, and the doctors. I had no choice but to trust and believe all would be well.

This was big stuff on such a little boy. He was two and a half, and we asked him if he knew what he was doing at the hospital. His response was, "owie" nodding his head with a grin and a smile. I have it all on video. I thought it would be wise to video from the day we left the house to the day we left the hospital, should he ever wonder what happened to him. It kept my mind occupied and my hands busy, so I had no time to think the worst.

One of the most challenging days in my life was the morning I gave my Adam to the nurses at the surgery doors, his little red cheeks, and the stoned look of wonder in his eyes, staring at me, looking confused as to what I was doing with him. They had given him an oral sedative to calm him about 30 minutes before we walked him down to surgery. It was clear; he was feeling no pain. He stared at me as the doors shut. The gridded glass and the tears in my eyes made his little face a blur. At this moment, I had no clue if I would ever see him again.

As we wandered the hallways and spent what seemed an eternity trying to keep ourselves busy, as it was a 4 or 5 hour surgery, we ended up back at the waiting room close to the OR. It was a horrible little room with no windows, two couches, a table separating them with a light and a phone on it. It was orange, an awful orange. This memory for me is profound for two reasons, my story and a story I was about to learn.

It was just Dan and myself, some time into our wait, as mom had Jordan out for a walk somewhere, that a young man came in and asked if we would mind if he could use the phone. This was a time when cell phones we not common. I did not overthink it said "sure" and scooted over to the other couch where Dan was sitting. In hindsight, we should have given him some privacy and left the room. We were too caught up in our own stuff to think common courtesy.

The phone call went something like this… "no, Jonathan is not doing well. After school, he came home, grabbed an apple, and went to deliver his papers on his bike with no helmet. He was hit by a car, and we are waiting for the doctors now. We will keep you posted. Thank you, yes, his faith is strong. We will continue to pray." Then he left the room—my heart in my throat, tears streaming down my cheeks.

A short time after, there was a hustle and bustle in the hallway just adjacent to the waiting room. I noticed a group of doctors and the young man and, I assumed his wife went into another room just down the hall. At that time, we decided we needed some air, coffee, or something. We were in that beautiful entrance of BCCH, admiring all the décor and design, making what is usually a sterile, uninviting space called a hospital into a playground, an inviting, safe place to bring children of all ages. I noticed the young man, Jonathan's dad, and his wife walk out the main doors, her head on his shoulder as he supported her with both arms with a somber air about them. It was a curious vision for me that sticks in my mind like yesterday, wondering how things were and where they were going. Perhaps they just needed a break too.

We made our way back to that room and patiently waited for the news that Adam had successfully come out of surgery, and all went well.

Eventually, we did get the news, and now we could go scrub and head into the ICU to be with him. He did not look like Adam but something that the staff calls Michelin (like the white tire guy on the ads ) babies. He was so puffy. I thought he looked like the Stay Puff Marshmallow Man from Ghostbusters. Apparently, this is standard post-op.

All was well; the machines, the people, tech, nurses, doctors, administrators, the ICU was an open hub of activity. This place did not stop. I was simply in awe of how it seemed to be a system of chaos. In the middle of the open room, beds on the peripheral walls, was the control center, the central station where all was organized. Behind the large desk was an even more giant whiteboard. Written on the whiteboard were grids with bed numbers and names, doctors, times, and a bunch of other information that meant nothing to me.

What did make sense to me was that Adam was in bed eight and Jonathan was in bed nine. It confused me as to why his parents were not at his bedside as he looked to be sleeping peacefully. Perhaps 13 or so and a beautiful young boy.

Later that day, I had just come back into the room and noticed that Jonathan's bed was empty. Mary, Adam's nurse, was wonderful, was attending to Adam, and I gently asked what happened to Jonathan. Her reply was, "his heart went to Toronto, his lungs went to… his kidneys went…" She said calmly; "you know his mom's mother was the first liver or kidney (I cannot quite remember) recipient in Vancouver years ago, so the decision, I suppose, was made with that in mind." Again, I was left speechless while tears streamed down my cheeks.

In reflection, I watched this family, going through an unimaginable story with grace and dignity, giving to strangers what our medical system has put in place to save someone's life who was in need. On my drivers' license, I now have it on record that I am an organ donor simply because of this profound experience. I believe if it were me, I could not have even come close to having handled it with such poise. I held my little Michelin man a little tighter those next few days, and I was humbled with the overwhelming gratitude that I felt that Adam only had what he had.

The following week or so went by quickly, progress being made every day, when we finally left the hospital with Adam and Jordan in our arms, balloons, gifts, cards, and love from so many. I promised that one day, somehow, someway, I would give back. Not just with money but with something. I just was not sure what it would be. It took about nine years for the opportunity to knock on my door, and I ran through it will full intention that I was going to fulfill that promise that I had made to myself so many years earlier.

Years later…

It was a sunny day in Vancouver, and I was enjoying her in all her glory. There is nothing quite like being on the water, on a beautiful boat enjoying laughter, sharing wine, and stories with old and new friends. I had received an invitation from a colleague who was in my office to join him and some of his friends on a Boat Cruise hosted by Sports Page, a local, late-night evening news broadcast that covered the days sporting events in 30 min. The invite came from a past NHL player and friend, Mark Lofthouse, hence the connection to the local sports show.

My reputation had preceded me regarding being a good organizer, getting things done, and no bullshit. At the time, the host of the show, Paul Carson, made his way over to me and introduced himself and proceeded to say, I hear you are good at organizing things. I said, ok, I can be, not sure where this was going. He explained that the guys at the show and the people at UTV were thinking about organizing their first-ever Sports Page Golf Classic, bringing together past and present athletes, raising money for charity, and having some fun in the process. I am good at fun! He wondered if I would consider joining the committee and help make it happen. In my naive boldness, my answer was sure, only if I get to call the charity. The answer was absolutely! Looking back at my attitude, I was surprised that I was welcomed at all, let alone with open arms with an anticipated excitement to get things underway.

My mind went immediately to BCCH, cardiology. Specifically Dr. LeBlanc, the surgeon that fixed Adam's heart many years ago. I intended to go directly to him and ask what he needed in his OR, anything, and you name it, I will do my best to get it for you. These were my thoughts, as I did not want to raise a bunch of money for it to go somewhere that I did not know or have passion for.

So, I approached Dr. LeBlanc (Jacque) and asked him to come to our committee with some thoughts. I will never forget the meeting that we had at the station where Jacque explained to us in painstaking doctor talk with exhibits that seemed to be of a foreign language, which bored me to tears. Nevertheless, I understood the machine he wanted would cost about 100K USD, and we did not have one in

Canada. It sounded like a good start to me, and I was off to the races.

Our first meeting was with Bert and Hans Koning (Koning's food suppliers, now known as Sysco) myself, Paul, and Nick Misisco (head of advertising at the time for UTV). It took about 10 minutes for me to tell my story and for Hans to look over at Bert with a nod of his head, told me to go tell my doctor to buy his machine. 100K spread over a 4-year commitment was what we walked out with that day, over the moon with excitement that we could do this!

We continued with our meetings, Chrysler, Seaboard life Insurance, and a list that was long. All got the mom's simple story on the committee with the son who had a couple of operations and wanted to buy some stuff for cardiology's operating room. I will never forget Paul coming to me one day saying they are not that happy about this whole thing. They, meaning Children's Hospital fundraising committee, I would expect, have different priorities for the money that was being raised, especially in the amounts we were raising. His simple answer was, "I will let you take that up with the mom on the committee that is spearheading this story because of her son." He never heard a complaint after that, nor did I ever hear from them. In the end, I believe we helped buy four machines for that OR, and we had a ton of fun doing it. What fond, beautiful memories, to be able to do something with a purpose has been one of the most fulfilling things I have done in my life to date.

Years later, I have lost time on this one. Dr. LeBlanc called me and invited me to come and watch a live correction and to see in real-time what a couple of the machines did in the OR that was a result of all the fundraising we had done. Let me begin this by saying I was completely honored by this jester, but taken aback. I cannot even look when my blood is being drawn. I get queasy at the sight of blood and needles. How on earth could I respectfully decline this offer. I could not.

So, one balmy summer afternoon dressed in my real estate clothing, high heels, et al. I was looking like I should be selling a million $ property in West Vancouver instead of going to watch an open-heart surgery, what was I thinking? I made my way down to BCCH. No clue what to expect, freaking out about what I was on my way to do and to watch.

I soon found myself standing at those very surgery doors with the gridded glass. I took a deep breath and took the step to the other side, seeing where and what, so many years ago, Adam had experienced after his scarey, stoned eyes left mine, and I turned and walked back down the hall we had just come from.

As I walked through, I heard commotion and busyness. I was directed to scrub and how to properly wash my hands. They put me in full greens, mask, booties, hat, and gown. I proceeded to the room adjacent to the wash station, where about 15 busy people were organizing an operating room with intention and experience. Again, organized chaos.

As I was standing in the corner trying not to get in the way, a nurse came over to me, introduced herself and proceeded to explain several things, and thanked me. First, she walked me over to a machine and explained that this machine kept the water that the medication ran through at a specific temperature. It had to be kept cold. Only a short time ago, they would have to run the water for hours in the summer months to get it cold enough to maintain the temperature needed to do this. The water lines in Vancouver's city were not buried deep enough to keep the water cold for the length of time that a patient needed to be sedated to perform such a lengthy surgery as an open-heart.

Next, she explained what I would hear, likened it to a chain saw noise, that would be the sternum being opened! Then she said I would smell something that I might think was burning, that again was the sternum being opened, OMG, then she pointed up at two TV monitors, she explained I could watch from there. Of course, my head was spinning all the while thinking I needed to run fast and get out of there. No way did I need nor want to watch, or did I want to experience any of this. I proceeded to explain to her I fainted at the sight of blood and needles. She looked at me like I had two heads and said, "ok, please stand over here because if you faint, none of us will be able to deal with you and you will not do any damage or be in the way over here." She abruptly walked away. I must have had a look of despair in my eyes as the anesthetist turned and said, what you are about to see today is nothing short of magnificent! I thought, what an unusual adjective to use for this situation.

The man of the hour, or the next four, walked in. Dr. LeBlanc greeted me with warmth and respect, introducing me to everyone and explaining my contributions and why a civilian dressed in 4" Manolo Blahnik's was standing in their OR. I was humbled. He introduced me to his patient, a little girl about five, as I recall. She was prepped and asleep on the table draped in green. Classical music played as the procedure got underway. I heard, I smelt, and I did not faint.

Dr. LeBlanc talking to me the whole time, small talk, how is business, the weather, how is Adam? Then he said, Kim, get over here! As I walked toward the table, full of fear of the unknown, the anesthetist graciously stepped aside, helped me up onto the step, and said, here is what I am talking about. Her little head was at my thighs as I peered over the drape and proceed to watch four hands, two brilliant surgeons working together as if they were doing something that was second nature, as seamless as breathing. I stood in AWE, speechless, watching nothing short of magnificent.

Dr. LeBlanc showed me what Adam's hole looked like. He showed me the pulmonary artery that was closed. Pulmonary stenosis is one of the four problems that make up the tetra; in the tetralogy of Fallot. Fallot is the doctor's name that discovered the defect. He showed me the Gore-Tex they used to repair them. The four and a half hours went by and I did not think once of how my shoes were so uncomfortable or even notice the time. Within a blink of an eye, it was over. Four and a half hours went by like nothing.

I stepped down off the box and thanked everyone and fully expressed my gratitude for having been so privileged to witness such an event, walked away, once again deer in headlights, and made my way home.

Years later, Jordan was diagnosed with Type one diabetes. He was 16, late for this type of diagnosis. Dan and I walked the hallways once again, only this time with Jordan. However, instead of turning right to 3G, the cardiology wing turned left to 3E, the diabetes wing. Similarly, spending time with a new fear and learning curve that the nurses and dietitians delivered with expertise, confidence, knowledgeable, kindness and patience. I was reminded that all would be well.

It is knowing that there is movement from the unknown to the understanding. It is knowing the fear that comes with that unknown will change with learning and education. *You do not know what you do not know* is such a profound concept. Thinking this can quiet my mind when the unknown and fear get the better of me, and gratitude is the action that keeps me on track. I will pause and be grateful and reflect on how lucky I am to have had boys that only had and have what they do.

Our hospital system, the nurses, doctors, the cleaning staff, every wheel and chassis make a hospital run. All this we have at our disposal in British Columbia and Canada everywhere. A privilege we pay for, yet still a privilege.

I bang my pots for you all. Thank you for your service and all you do! I am ever humbled and grateful.

**Kim Beck**

"The perfect world is created
when the mind is free to see it."

**BYRON KATIE**

# FIVE

## A Love Letter to Myself

### A PATH TO FORGIVENESS

You were three years old when you learned to be ashamed of yourself. A playful tickle game turned into something else; you were paralyzed by it. The touching was uncomfortable, and it hurt. You were so confused, and it felt like you were being punished, for what you didn't know.

Deep inside, you knew it was wrong, yet you said nothing, just whimpered and cried softly. You were so young, yet you felt ashamed. Why didn't you scream for them to stop? It was out of your control. It was destiny for who you were to become. A seed had been planted for what you would believe yourself to be and what you felt you deserved from life.

When you are young, the lessons come fast and furious, bringing avalanches of emotion too complex for a young mind to comprehend. You were learning and forming the lens from which you would view this life. Sadly, you learned that adults are not there to protect you, support you or believe in you. In a time when you were the most frightened, you felt ashamed, abandoned, and betrayed. In the darkest, horrific moments of despair, you did not know. You couldn't imagine anything beyond that moment. You had no idea the joy that life would bring to you. You didn't know it then, but you were loved, and you were safe.

A few months after that appalling and cruel incident in the basement of your home, you fell down the stairs while sneaking to watch late night TV with your Dad and suffered a concussion. Almost a year later, you were playing on the monkey bars in the park when you slipped off, hitting your head on the metal bars as you fell, again suffering a concussion. This time your head split open, and you were bleeding. You developed amblyopia, or lazy eye, which was treated with patch therapy, daily eye drops, eye exercises, and multiple surgeries.

You were an awkward, skinny, little two-headed three year-old, but you finally had your parents' attention, support and what felt like love.

You've always loved being alone. You used to hide in the bathroom at night while your family was sleeping, standing on the toilet on your tippy toes so you could peak out into the dark, quiet prairie night. In those moments, the vastness of the world was overwhelming, and you were in awe of the stars and the giant, never-ending dark navy sky. One night a rush of warmth and comfort filled your spirit. You stared at that one bright star, believing that it was a sign that someone somewhere loved you and you were going to be ok. No matter what happened, you were going to be ok. The universe was speaking to you. You were loved, and you were safe.

There were many nights where you hid in your bedroom, covers over your head, sometimes hiding under the bed, while your parents shouted at each other. Through the loud voices, you heard sounds of things breaking and chaos until it was eerily silent. It was then that that ringing in your ears began and has not stopped since. You didn't sleep those nights, waiting for it to stop, begin again, or for the sound of your Dad quietly knocking on your bedroom window wanting you to go to the locked back door to let him in.

One night it was raining so hard against your bedroom window that you didn't hear your Dad knocking. You heard something, and it frightened you. You pulled the covers over your head and covered your ears tightly with your little hands, squeezing your eyes shut, willing it to stop. Something gave you the courage to peak out from under the blankets and look at the window. Then you saw him, your Dad, tapping lightly on the window so that only you could hear. He was drenched from the rain with an incredibly vulnerable and desperate look on his face. For the first time in your life, your heart broke. It felt like you were exploding from the inside. You knew that feeling. You knew how he felt. The pain was so intense you could barely breathe, and you thought you could never forgive yourself for leaving your Dad out alone in the rain. You knew how it felt to be invisible.

When you were six years old, you were walking home from the park and noticed an unfamiliar, little blue car in front of your house, packed up to the windows. There was an RCMP car in the driveway. You walked into your living room, where your Mom, Dad, your sister, and your brother, and a policeman sat in silence as you approached. The policeman asked you, "Do you know why I'm here?" You shook your head no, but you knew. Your intuition was strong, and you knew how to listen to it and believe in it. You had learned how to talk to and listen to the universe.

That day that you came home to the strange car in front of your house and the policeman in your living room, you abandoned your Dad. Your Mom took you, your brother, and your sister to live in the city. Your Mom loved you and your brother and sister very much. She wanted a better life for her kids and herself. She was simply doing the best she could, with what she knew, in that moment. Still, you were loved, and you were safe.

The next time you saw your Dad, you were walking home from school, and you passed by a car with the driver side door slightly ajar. As you walked past, you heard his voice: "Hey! Are you just going to walk right past your dear old Dad?" Your heart stopped as you turned around in confusion. There was that face again, breaking your heart. Your Dad knew how much you loved him. Every one of those times that you thought you broke his heart; it was your heart that was breaking. His heart filled with joy at the sight of you. He never felt abandoned; he felt unworthy.

You didn't know that for almost a year after your Mom took you away that your Dad was in and out of rehab as he struggled with depression and alcoholism. When he stopped going to rehab, he went looking for his kids. He knew the best way to hurt your Mom was to take her kids from her. So that is exactly what he did. Your Mom was powerless, and she had no means to fight him, and the laws to protect her were different then. Losing her kids devastated her beyond what you can ever imagine. Still, you were loved, and you were safe.

You needed surgery on your eye when you were seven years old. You were staying in a strange place with your Dad, and you had just started to doze off when you felt a hand rubbing your arm, whispering for you to wake up. Your eye was covered with a large gauze patch, your vision was blurry, and your mind was in a fog. Still, you knew it was her from her sweet, fresh, familiar scent and loving touch. When your Mom lifted you into her arms, you instantly fell into a peaceful sleep. Suddenly you were awakened to find your parents screaming at each other, and your Dad was tugging at your arms to release you from your Mom's embrace. The struggle was frightening and painful. You wanted to cry. You wanted to yell at them to stop. Again, you were voiceless and heard only that familiar ringing in your ears. It was getting louder and louder.

After you moved back with your Dad, he spent very little time at home. You would ride your bike through the night looking for him. Sometimes you would find him drunk or passed out in the tiny apartment in the back of his furniture store. Other times you would find him in the one bar in your tiny town. On good days you found him in the clubhouse at the golf course, laughing with his golf buddies, smelling of beer and pickled eggs. When you found him, you crawled into his lap, laid your head on his chest, and fell asleep to the vibrations of his voice, his breath, his laughter, and the beat of his heart.

Your Dad tried to take care of you and your siblings by hiring housekeepers to live with you, to take care of you and the house. They were mostly kind and made life a little easier, though all remained strangers. None of them lasted more than a few months. There was the uptight, extremely religious, and easily agitated one, the one who thought she believed she could fly and would ask you and your sister to plant marshmallows in the front yard to grow marshmallow trees. The one who would make out in her boyfriend's car parked outside your house for hours until one day she was taken back to the mental hospital she had escaped from.

Later you learned that the "housekeepers" and visits from your Grandma were all reactions to your Dad learning that child services had been alerted and were considering taking you, your brother, and your sister away. Still, you were loved. You were safe.

Elementary school was difficult. You felt strange and isolated. Your divorced parents were an anomaly in your small town. Yet your Dad was revered because he was a former professional baseball player and held the world record holder for the longest throw in baseball.

He was also pitied and feared for his struggles to adjust to this his new life and his new identity. No longer the star, effortlessly moving through life watched and admired by adoring fans. When he looked at you with his sad, lost hazel eyes, it broke your heart, and you wanted to fix him. You idolized him and loved him deeply, always.

For years, you seldom saw your Mom. She would promise to come get you, and you would wait, sitting in the living room on the floor looking out the large window to the front, waiting for the little blue car to pull into the gravel driveway. The afternoon would pass, the sun would set, and it eventually got dark. Still, there you sat, waiting, forgotten. Being unwanted is a heavy burden. Still, you were loved, and you were safe.

You spent more time alone while your brother and sister were at sleepovers, vacationing with friends, and traveling for sports. Your Dad was rarely at home, and you gave up looking for him. Now that you were older, you came to understand that he didn't want to be found. Being alone was what you knew. You were seven years old when you learned to shop, to cook, and take care of yourself. You learned to be resilient and to survive!

The summer before 8th grade, you and your sister moved to Calgary to live with your Mom again. This time without your brother. You never considered how hard it would be to move to the city and to a new school. That first day at school was more than you ever could have imagined. You felt like an alien. People stared and pointed and whispered as you walked through the halls and to your classes. You were used to being invisible. You were not used to this!

Your heart sank when everyone was asked to find a locker partner. You prayed that everyone would pick someone, and you would be the one left and given mercy by being assigned a locker on your own. That's how it always happened in the past when your class was told to find a partner or one of the kids was made "captain" and called out the names of the people they wanted on their team. You always stood quietly, being invisible until, by default, you would be left out of the game or given a consolation prize.

To your surprise, a pretty girl with long, curly dark hair and beautiful blue eyes approached you. She smiled, looking directly into your eyes, and said, "Hi, wanna be my locker partner?!" In that single, simple moment, you felt validated, and you finally knew the joy of being vulnerable. Nothing had felt so right. Those words that you didn't know your heart longed for, "will you be my..." filled your heart with joy. It was wonderful to feel wanted and worthy. In an instant, you found your best friend, your shining light. You were going to be ok. That love and light gave you faith. It was the beginning of your journey to forgiveness, releasing your shame and moving closer to the beautiful life you deserve.

All that happened to you in the past made you more, not less. That sad, ashamed little girl does not define you. She is a part of you, and you will carry her with you always. She needs your love, understanding, and, mostly, your forgiveness. You know, there is no need for forgiveness unless there is blame, and you've always blamed one person, yourself.

The Universe always has and will always take care of you. You are seen, heard, and understood, and you were sent to this earth to help others feel seen, heard, and understood. You are loved, you are safe, and you are a gift! You were born a perfect limitless soul, and you are not bound by your circumstances. Nothing about what has happened in your life has, or ever can, change that. You are loved, completely, utterly, and beyond worldly imagination!

**"The path to forgiveness and healing is only a thought away."**

**Kandis Wells**

"There is no greater gift you can give or receive than to honor your calling. It's why you were born. And how you become most truly alive."

**OPRAH WINFREY**

SIX

# Own Your Life to Become Finally Free

## THE WOMAN WHO MIRACULOUSLY SURVIVED AND LEARNED WHAT TRUE FREEDOM MEANS

It was March 18th, 2014, when I silently drove with my then husband to the hospital with a quickly filled bag in the back of the car. It's a ride I will never forget. I looked at him after 10 minutes of tense silence and said, 'I'm not ready to die yet.'

That morning I had been in another hospital to visit a neurosurgeon because, for a week, I'd been feeling off and kept telling my doctor that something wasn't well inside me. Disgraced and annoyed, he told me to stop bothering all the doctors, don't act so dramatically, and just go lie in bed for three weeks with my flu. Defeated I accepted his words and went home to lie in my bed.

Three hours later, my doctor called me and asked if I was alone. My body froze. "I will be at your home in twenty minutes." While my husband rushed back home from doing groceries, she told me they'd found an extreme amount of white blood cells in my blood that morning and that this indicated acute leukemia. The only thing that came to mind was an image of children with bloated bald heads. She gave me five minutes to pack my bag and asked me if I preferred an ambulance or our own car.

So off we drove. Into the unknown. Our three young kids were at the daycare and in school. Only to find out that evening that their mother had an aggressive life threatening disease and would be gone for about three months.

Little did we know, that turned out to be just the beginning of a long journey. Thanks to inhuman treatments, extremely high doses of chemo, the initial life threat went away. While looking into death's eyes twice, being completely burned to the ground, undergoing a high-risk stem-cell transplantation, and almost succumbing to the consequences of my stem-cell rejection, I faced an abnormally long list of complications, depressions, and many dark nights of the soul. I can say that after three years of continuous treatments, I survived.

Later I heard doctors say, "We know no one else who could have survived this amount of bad luck." I remember thinking, I just did what I needed to do in order to survive this. I actually had decided day one that I would survive. Chances are, that's the main reason I'm still here.

**Our signature in life**

From where I stand now, knowing everything I've come to learn, having been through that journey with cancer, having seen many people go through difficult times in a different way, and now also guiding other people through that journey of conscious living with cancer - I can say I truly believe that **it is how we live through those moments, that defines us.** It's our signature in life.

How we live is how we deal with our difficulties. Facing it in the eye, moving around it, trying to control it, give up on it, or fight it. Some live consciously. Others try to escape from reality and let it pass by as much as possible. We all do this differently, and there should no judging involved. We all have good reasons to act how we act. It's all part of a bigger story.

When I got my diagnosis that day, I had already developed a deep connection with my higher self due to years of personal development, so I could consciously choose to take the path of least resistance and, therefore, highest chances to get through it. Others carry on with rage, frustration, and fight-mode. And there are others who say they want to stay alive, but when I ask them, they can't even find a deep desire inside themselves to stay alive.

I remember the moment where we were waiting for the first blood results which would judge my chance of life - how I had a vision of a crossroads where the left road would lead to disappointment, anger, resistance, and suffering. I saw it would be a very difficult and arduous road. The road to the right was one where I immediately accepted the situation as it was, went through all the difficulties, pain, and horror, but without resistance. I remember this moment very brightly, and it took me exactly 21 minutes to decide which road I would choose. I choose to go right, and in hindsight, this might have been the moment where I chose LIFE as the outcome.

Of course, there are also the circumstances like blood levels and statistics, but I feel the intention to live is equally as important. I miraculously survived with a 20% chance. Later I almost died of complications of my treatments. So there wasn't a high percentage for me on paper. I know others have way higher chances and don't survive it. So there's more involved than just chemo and good luck.

**Not average**

You might see this as a huge story, which it obviously is. But honestly, to me, it's just one of the bigger chapters of a life of 'non-average-events'.

As a child, I walked around with the heaviness of not fitting in, being bullied, sexual harassment, and that sense of not-belonging went on into my adult life. I was lucky also to have great moments where I felt seen, connected, and gifted. So there was a place inside me where I just knew there's love, and I am meant for greatness. I think this pulled me through many years.

But still, the road was rocky... I had many losses in friendship, looked quite outgoing and social but felt pretty alone most of the time because I missed real connections. I had many bad experiences with boyfriends. While being desperate to be loved, I allowed criminals, alcoholics, and abusers into my life, all 'in the name of love.' I had my first burnout when I was 14 years old, along with my mother, who was ill in that period; my second, third and fourth during my twenties. For as long as I can remember, I haven't had a week without having pain in my body.

When I gave birth to my first child, it was a horrific miscalculation of the nurse that led to a very traumatic process of giving birth. Of course, the doctor told me not to be so emotional and that I was wrong with my observation that things weren't good.

I say 'of course' because this too is part of the story of my life. Me having clarity of what's going on inside my body, speaking out and being silenced and judged by doctors and experts, to finally find out I was right all along. That pattern comes with me until this day. It's something that I still hate, for it comes with an immense sense of hopelessness and loneliness - but I managed to not let it ruin my strength anymore. I was a sensitive kid and young woman. I am still a sensitive woman. The difference is that now I stand by myself, knowing that being sensitive is a God given gift, not a curse or weakness.

In my second pregnancy, I was blessed with twins. Their birth process was even more horrible, and we ended up separated in two hospitals. I could write a book alone about how horrific that was. Them cutting my artery with the first twin so I was bleeding empty ('No miss, please stop complaining, there's nothing wrong') and making a mistake with the epidermal for the second twin which resulted in a terrible treatment to help me recover from that. To end up not hearing or seeing the second boy after birth for days and knowing that the brothers were separated into different hospitals was beyond heartbreaking.

By now, you can imagine, when I was diagnosed with leukemia, and we went into this process - no one around me, including me, was surprised I had the acute and aggressive version. No one was surprised I had an abnormal amount of abnormal side-effects and disease during my process of healing from leukemia (from a wrongly operated foot to an inflamed pericardium, to temporary loss of memory and speech, and many many more on the list). No one was surprised that the procedures pained me much more than the average patient. In no case was I an average patient, but I was reminded daily for years that I wasn't - as if there was something wrong with me in my way of going through this unpaved road.

**When you start believing it**

What I notice, when I look back, I see how people around me started with little sentences like 'with you, nothing goes normal,' 'with you everything is always more intense than with others', 'of course with you it never goes easy,' 'with other people it goes like this, but with your abnormal reactions we don't know…' You have no idea how strong those lines are. How deep they go. How quick and fierce you start believing them. You start saying it yourself before someone else can say it. With an uncomfortable laugh - I guess because you start shaming yourself for feeling weak without being weak. And in time, you become this shadow of who you truly are.

**When abnormal becomes your normal**

My list of unreal heavy experiences is long. Sometimes when I share it with new friends, they have to breathe deeply throughout my story. And I cannot blame them. The thing is, to me, it's my normal. Or better, it was my normal. I got to learn that I am not supposed to carry all my weight with me all along. I got so extremely resilient and good in carrying on while having all this shit-load of heaviness on my shoulders. But I got to realize that should be the standard. It took me years to change that in my system, and honestly, it's still there some days where I need to remind myself that I'm worth living in ease and joy. That it's my birthright to be free and feel joy (without carrying ten suitcases of heavy shit along).

## My resilience-muscle

I had quite some opportunities to build my resilience muscle throughout life, and especially during my journey with cancer and everything that came with it. It's about these moments where I endured more than I thought I'd be able to endure anymore. Over and over again. It blows my mind how heavy this goes and how far it brought me.

Resilience to me has everything to do with surrendering, the ability to be in the now, and moving through unimaginable difficulties with the least amount of resistance that's possible. Because you know every ounce of resistance that you will bring to it, will enlarge your suffering to unmeasured heights.

After the cancer journey, life still brings me enough moments to train and use my 'resilience muscle'. I noticed that to other people, I kind of became the woman who could endure anything with grace, 'you are strong, you can deal with this'. Also, I discovered through deep healing sessions that I unconsciously was being a resilient 'warrior'. So it made me think about what resilience actually is, how it helps you and where it starts working against you.

I feel it's important to share two important things I know now when it comes to resilience:

First of all, we all have the ability to bear and endure much more than we imagine to be possible. I have it, and so do you. It's incredible what we can handle physically, emotionally, mentally, and spiritually. Even when you feel you enter the end of your ability to keep on going, there's more ability to hold it coming forward.

Secondly, however, being a resilient 'warrior' is the best way to get through such difficult moments. I noticed that even that quality has a downside. Being proud of our capability to deal with heavy things can also become a prison and therefore holding you back from true inner freedom. After we've built this resilience muscle and survived unbearable things (mostly more than once) - we unconsciously tend to hold a 'batch of honor' on how well we master the art of resilience. This will keep us stuck in a repeating pattern of encountering circumstances that ask for resilience. True freedom lies beyond that.

**The pain of not-belonging**

Not-belonging has been a common thread in my life. I've felt this sense of not belonging in my childhood, while I became a teenager, an adult, a grown up with study, workplaces, circle of friends (or lack of real good friends). At first, it doesn't have so much to do with my cancer story, right? Although, also in the hospital, I felt most of the time as an alien between other creatures, while doctors never seemed to speak or understand my language - and of course, I recognized that burning feeling of being alienated from previous experiences, and I had to be careful to not question my existence time and time again.

The reason I want to mention it here is this is larger than me and my story. Not-belonging is a common thread in many people's lives. I know this from people of all kinds of surroundings and all layers of society. You know what? 99% of my clients know this sense of not belonging! So, of course, that made me think how it's all connected. It's a super important piece of the puzzle in what I got to learn how this works (and why it's important).

However, this feeling of not-belonging is super painful and unwanted; it also made me who I am today. It's also connected to the natural longing to grow and become more and more of myself. Like 'If I don't belong with them (or them or them), then who am I? If I were to belong to myself, who am I? What does that look like?"

I see it in my own journey, where I couldn't wait to come on this journey of inner growth around 18 years old. I also recognize this in like-minded souls, who all share this feeling of not-belonging. I see it in their ability and eagerness to grow internally, do the inner work, and rise up to become more and more who they truly are. Becoming more connected to your authentic being, your own truth, will immediately make you more connected. Connected to yourself, your unique path in life, to like-minded souls. It's like you're stepping into that place into the bigger picture of Life (not your life) that already belongs to you. Where you already belong.

From this painful feeling of not-belonging, for me and many others comes forth a drive to find your own path, discover other places, looking for that moment where things do click, and you feel 'home'. Sometimes that other 'home' or feeling of belonging is in the presence of other people. Sometimes it's in a state of being, sometimes it's in specific environments (at the sea, in the mountains). Of course, it is not about those external circumstances at all. It's about how we relax and are able to lean in into those specific circumstances.

Belonging is in me. It's in you. It's about finding those circumstances to be able to relax into becoming you and connect deeply with yourself and your purpose in life. Slowly I started to find out what those are to me.

**Becoming who you are**

It needs to be said that, however, I learned a lot out of walking my path with this feeling of not-belonging (like getting to deeply know myself, finding my inner power, and trusting my inner wisdom). It's not a given thing that one gains from suffering. I deeply believe every crisis or challenge holds a gift for me - that's my default. Not in the suffering itself, but in the layers, you'll come through by consciously working through that challenge. Without that attitude, I might just have suffered a lot, full stop. So, of course, one needs to consciously take that opportunity. Without you intentionally taking this opportunity, it's just flat sand doing nothing. To me, it's clear that it's important to see this bigger picture when you want to grow in life, like why would you even want to look at a crisis like this?

However, I'm talking about quite heavy life stories here. I need to confess I totally love the process of inner growth. I cannot imagine a life without it! Oh my, sometimes it's a roller coaster with highs and lows. But it's also life flowing through your veins! I feel Life just becomes more beautiful and enjoyable as I let myself grow.

Growing as a person means: coming back to who you truly are. In a world where we have to be, do and have everything, it can be quite challenging to be who you already are. However, it took me decades to figure out who I was and who not. I feel I'm still and forever on this journey. It's like a lifelong spiral where we move through different layers of ourselves, becoming more and more pure and authentic. Getting to know who you truly are and practicing being YOU is challenging but not impossible. More importantly, it's an amazing ride if you surrender to the process, are willing to get out of your comfort zone, be messy and imperfect on your way to elevation, and reach new levels of inner freedom.

**Gifts in disguise**

Whenever I doubt my rollercoaster path of inner growth, I just have to imagine myself ten years from now, and nothing would have changed - to know I'm all in. Imagine how would that feel? How would it be if you would stay exactly like you're now for eternity? Exactly, stagnation and boredom. It's definitely not honoring the gifts with which we've been brought into this life.

Throughout the course of my life, I learned that my true 'gifts' that are connected to my purpose are not the talents that were visible from the outside, like playing the violin or being great in art. My gifts lie so much deeper. And they came to me through challenges. It was not the challenges itself, it was what it opened up inside of me, which led me to my true gifts and purpose. For example, I'm exceptionally well at holding space for others' process, hearing what's not said, lovingly pinpoint one's pain point for them to grow. This is nothing like playing violin or creating art. These are gifts that I gained by living this exact life, in this exact constellation, with my exact unique impact and purpose. It's my mission to stop the silent suffering and help others find inner freedom and enter this life where life is actually enjoyable. Why? Because it's all, I didn't experience. We all teach what we need the most.

**Unique backpacks**

Of course, there is the big *'Why?'* Why do we have to go through all these traumas and life changing events? After studying human behavior, spiritual psychology and psychosynthesis, systemic work, and many more for over 20 years, I've found my own understanding of how this works. And it helps me to move through challenging times with much more ease and grace and definitely less resistance. I wouldn't know what I had to do without having such an understanding of the bigger picture, so I feel I need to share it here with you.

Let's say we all come into this life with a little invisible backpack, filled with life lessons and specific pieces of karma that are waiting to be resolved. These are things that haven't been resolved in previous generations, and if you would, in previous lives. We as Soul know what we get ourselves into before we choose this life. The family we're born into, with all its own drama and dynamic. The life-path we will walk, including all highs and lows.

I've come to learn that we have a choice there, right before we say yes to this life's journey. Meaning, whenever we are in this life experiencing trauma, this is something we consciously choose to experience as a Soul. I know this is a hard pill to swallow. It took me years to fully understand and accept this.

Since I do, it takes the heavy weight off of all my lows in life. At the moment, they are still horrific and heavy to experience, but there's also a layer where I fully trust the process, as I know there's a bigger plan to this life - and I said yes to all of it up front. The important thing is, we as spirits in this human body with ego and mind and all personal stuff going on don't have a clue of the bigger picture. We think we do, but we don't. Really. So that means there's less to control and more to live.

It took me years to figure out how this is all connected in the bigger picture. Our gifts (disguised as challenges) come to us through life lessons, though trauma, through challenges along your path. They are accumulated through the family you've been born into, the teachers and (lack of) friends you had, through the way you grew up and became an adolescent, found your own adult life, and maybe build your own family. It's a complex combination of circum-stances, culture, specific people around you, your personality, and events that happen on your journey. Besides that, not everything needed to happen in your own life, to be of influence in your life. We carry energy and DNA with us from seven generations before us. So, it's a complex reality. Nothing stands alone. And nothing is what it looks like at first. This also means that your story, with a series of little and big traumatic events you survived, are just chap-ters in your life. Chapters that show you the direction where your lessons need to be learned and integrated.

**Loving my story**

I know it's easy to dislike the events that happened and are still happening in your life that we consider challenges or worse. But honestly, during this whole journey of life discovery, I learned that it's our life stories that hold our truth. My exact life story, the exact freaking series of events, holds my truth. It carries my gifts. These life lessons, challenges are not who I am. These are just chapters in my book of Life and are there for a reason that only can be seen when you've lived through them. It's not about the events itself. It's the lessons, insights, and strength that came from it.

These things that are happening in my life are not happening TO me. They are happening FOR me. These things are NOT a punishment. I haven't done something wrong to deserve them. I am not a loser for having so many sad stories in my life. It is NOT what defines me!

It's just how my backpack is filled with lessons to contribute to the evolution of mankind. And it's all that I've said 'Yes' to before I came into this life.

By living through these lessons, by unpacking these task packages during life, we not only set free our own livelihood, freedom, and happiness, we also set free our whole family system and pave the way for our children and grandchildren to not come into this same system again.

**Is it all about the shitty moments in life?**

So, is learning in life all about crappy moments? No! It was also moments of success, happiness, big leaps forward in my life that taught me many important lessons - and I would say they also belong to my metaphorical backpack. Life is a continuous journey where we change from perspective. What seems like success or happiness in one moment doesn't mean later in life you can't look at it while learning many lessons. For example, my marriage that gave me everything I was looking for at that time and was a gift from heaven also let me unpack many life lessons disguised as challenges. This is the same for successes in my business. I've learned so much from the road to those moments, like coming out of my comfort zone, overcoming the fear of not being enough, dealing with internal voices 'What will they think?' or 'Who am I to...'. And also there, the perspective changes constantly. What once was a challenge or big win later seems to be irrelevant in the context of steps. It's in the high and the low where we learn and grow.

**We can't heal what we don't feel**

It was tremendously helpful for me to learn along the way what trauma actually is. It took the horror away from it when it was time for healing. What happens when you experience trauma or hardship, you freeze your energy. This happens totally naturally and unconsciously. It's our amazing way to survive. However, I honor that amazing system. I don't want frozen energy to be who I am and how I live. We feel so contracted, lost, and fearful because it's frozen. For me, it helps to look at this huge, immense feeling as 'just energy' that is frozen. It becomes less scary to me. It's like water in a frozen river. We need to unfreeze it for the water to move with natural grace through the river (life).

What was also helpful is the insight that a trauma is not about the event itself. It's about how it made you feel inside. It's not that we need to deep dive years into that specific event or the people who were involved. For my time in the hospital, I don't need to relive those hundred thousand scary moments. I need to connect to how it made me feel inside. Which emotions, deep fears, and triggers were activated.

And I know, feeling all the feelings can be frightening up front. Now that I've been there, I need you to know that the fear of the fear is always bigger than the feeling itself. Meaning trying not to go to that place, to not let something happen because you are so fearful of what might happen there (for real, when you bring it down to the essence, it's mostly the fear to be outcast or die). But once you've actually entered that space, without exception, this is always way less scary than assumed in front. I know this from my own experience and see it with all my clients. You want to get out of that terrible feeling, but the quickest way out is in. Actual emotion doesn't take much time or effort. It's deep for a few seconds or minutes, and then it transforms into another energy. Fear becomes calmness and hope. Loneliness becomes a deep sense of connection to a higher source, etc.

In order to live a free life, feel happy, be creative and resourceful, we need to heal and unblock what's holding us back and is keeping us stuck from moving into a better place. So there's no way around it, we need to feel in order to heal.

**My unpacked gifts in disguise**

For me, I unpacked many lessons during my time in the hospital and during life after hospital (which is a life itself!). Also, when it comes to long term bullying, sexual harassment, burnout, depression, divorce, moving through another country, and more, I unpacked many life lessons, gifts in disguise.

I learned that when you're able to distance yourself from the actual events, and you regularly look with a bird's eye to your life - you start to see how it's all connected. What threads are woven throughout your life? How seemingly different events end up to be about the same deep lesson, there for you until you're able to fully unpack all layers of it.

The actual list of life lessons I've gained until now, being 44 years young, is too long to fit into this chapter. But I'll give you a short list of the lessons learned during having and recovering from cancer. This might help you to figure out some of your life lessons:

*I had to be into my body and stop living from the head.* The years before the cancer had made me a visionary but also a controller. There was much trauma that made me move out of my body, into my head. I see this all the time, mainly with women. We live from the breast up and in our heads. Due to the many physical interventions, I realized I either stick being in the traumatized body while enlarging the trauma, or I would learn to actually be and stay present with every needle or worse that came into my body. I consciously chose the last and am grateful for it because now I know in order to create more than only dreams, to actually manifest my gifts, I need to be able to make it physical and be able to embody it. The stream of intuition, guidance, inner wisdom that comes to me from being IN my body is incredible.

*True freedom lies within you.* Nothing is more powerful than entering the field of inner freedom. And you'll enter it the moment you realize it's not the circumstances that imprison you. It's your mind that does.

*I am not guilty, and I am not abandoning my children.* I had to deal with a lot of guilt towards my children, mostly towards my oldest, who consciously experienced all of it. Mommy who was suddenly ripped away from their lives. The fear of saddling them with trauma from a critically ill mother and all the scary appearances that I got from chemo and heavy medication. Their fall from paradise where they know that everything can just be finite. The trust I must place into their father, who is amazing but just not their mother. I had to learn that this is beyond my control and that also they had said yes to their lives, including growing up with a mother with a life threatening disease. It's just the moment that you know for sure that they will get bumps and bruises by growing up in my presence, in this family - which was just hard to accept.

*It was in the middle of the worst period of chemo, where I found the power of authenticity.* Imagine, I was literally and figuratively stripped down, naked. No hair on my head, no strength in my body. In loss of any possibility to have things under control. No clothes to hide behind, no masks to wear, not even an ego to steal the show. I was so beaten down by this horrific medicine (and yes, my savior as well) that there was nothing left but essence. Pure essence. Raw. Real. Nothing concealing. In other words, it was revealing my true self. I remembered a clear moment where it hit me. This, here right now, is where people see me, my strength, and deeply appreciate that I'm here and sharing my truth. And it comes naturally and effortlessly to me.

*Going through an intense journey on the edge of life and death connected me to my (already) strong desire to live.* To live to the fullest. I became more aware that this actually is MY life, and I'm not honoring it by living just a life, or just a little of my life. I need to live it to the fullest, meaning fully stepping into my own being, own my story, and find and follow my own path.

I encourage you to actually make a list for yourself. It's super helpful to write about it, reflect on it, let old stuff like guilt and blame go, and feel strong and proud about it. Don't make it perfect. Work on it from time to time.

**Essential ingredients**

The beautiful thing about surviving big things is that you can look back and see what got you there. I couldn't have done this without true and raw connection with people around me, feeling a sense of urgency to change this moment around, enough self-love to want to be present at the other side, connection to a higher source, the ability to surrender to the process and stop trying to control it and a big dose of resilience.

**Bold choices with ease and joy**

Since I've recovered from the leukemia and the treatments to help me stay alive, I went back to my 'normal' life, which of course, wasn't normal anymore. I had to figure out where my actual path would lead from there.

During this whole process, I learned a lot about finding and following my path. I gained so much connection to my own path and an increasing trust that if I were to be brave and choose that path, I would be guided along the way. Something that feels so true to your path and comes from within cannot be wrong. I won't say it has been easy, but it was the right decision. And there may be a lesson for all: whatever feels right doesn't necessarily feel easy.

And so it happened that once I got back on my feet after surviving leukemia and all the horror that came with that, I knew I had to leave my marriage, and a year later, I moved with my kids from The Netherlands to Ibiza in Spain.

You need to know that making these bold choices was not to run away from what's not good, but walking towards where I deep down feel I belong. Of course, these were no little steps, but big leaps, and the beauty was that it came so strongly from within me that I felt confident and (scared as hell but) ready to face whatever consequences that would have.

Of course, there were many reactions and opinions. Around the divorce, the reactions were 'what's wrong with the marriage,' and my answer was 'my path lies beyond this marriage, so staying here means not honoring my path'. Towards the movement to another country within the scope of a half year, the reactions were 'Oh my God, you are so brave!' and 'Where did you get the courage to do this?' and my answer was 'I can take these big leaps with ease and joy because I'm guided from within, and it only makes sense to follow my own path now I found it'.

It might have been helpful in both cases that I have looked death in the eye twice and felt I didn't have to lose any time to fully LIVE, but honestly, we're all capable of making these kinds of decisions if we're willing to own our desire to follow our own unique path and take what comes with it.

**Truly free & unstoppable**

This whole journey through life until here made me realize that the best possible place we can guide ourselves into is a place where we consciously choose every day to be free, authentic, and know that we are the creator of our lives. To be kind towards ourselves and others who also are on their journey through life.

My story holds my truth. It's my blessing. It's not despite but because of our journey with all these lessons that we become truly free and unstoppable creators. This goes for all of us, as it does for me:

*Freedom* arises where I stopped living my life for others, found and followed my own path, and created a strong foundation of inner freedom inside myself. I became **unstoppable**, where I stop over-working and proving myself, let go of perfectionism and stop filling the gap of my lonely heart. Instead, I became authentic, coming from the heart and finding my own rhythm.

I am the *creator* of my life. I decide what route I choose and what I let go of. I do this when I make the experience of fully being alive a priority and welcome joy, playfulness, and creativity into my life. It's then when my strength becomes even more powerful because it comes from within.

**Was it all worth it? Yes.**

This whole journey through life (and I'm not even at the end!) showed me what's important and how I could connect to who I truly am. This feeling of not belonging taught me everything about real connection. Becoming a warrior taught me that being a warrior is amazing, but not true freedom. Throughout working through many trauma's from my life. and from generations before, taught me how if we all do our own inner work, we're healing and evolving the collective - and at the same time creating a free and enjoyable life for ourselves.

I can honestly say now that I see my journey through cancer as a God given gift. I truly became a nicer person by it, for myself and for people around me. I am so much more healthy now emotionally, mentally, spiritually, and physically - although I live every day with the emotional and physical leftovers from it. There's no day that I don't have pain that or feel tired. I still need to go to hospitals and healers, and I still encounter new challenges that ask for even more resilience. The life-after cancer will never leave me. I'm in it for life.

But I live. I LIVE. I am loving the fact that I am alive. I am able to see my children grow, now ages twelve, nine, and nine. I get to choose to follow my own path. I get to breathe in pure air and experience the wonders of nature. I get to express myself in art, writings, and love. And I know I'm here for a reason - to teach and guide others about life. On how to stop suffering and start living; how to enter the field of inner freedom and start actually enjoying life!

**Leontine Boxem**

"Just as there is no warning for childbirth, there is no preparation for the sight of a first child. There should be a song for women to sing at this moment or a prayer to recite. But perhaps there is none because there are no words strong enough to name that moment."

**ANITA DIAMANT**

SEVEN

## How I became the Mom to Moms

IT TAKES A VILLAGE TO RAISE A KID ... YOU ARE NOT
ALONE.

It all began in the spring of my son's junior year. I remember being at the school, chatting with another mom about how our kids would be in their senior year coming up, and preparing myself for the ups and downs of letting go and excitement for when my son graduated. I was blessed to have a career that I absolutely loved as a fitness and wellness coach, and I felt like my career was going in the exact direction I wanted. My husband and I were starting to wonder what we would do after my son graduated.

All this wonder and vision of our future changed with a simple phone call. I received a phone call asking me if I would take care of a little boy. A family member recommended me as someone who could take care of a 13-month-old little boy who had been removed from his parents and was in foster care. After a lot of discussion between my husband and me, and a conversation with my son, we said yes. I was already a mom and thoroughly enjoyed it, so I thought, how hard can it be? I'm not confident about many things, but the one thing I was confident about was that I was a good mom. I naively thought that it was going to be easy. After a lot of conversations with the caseworkers and a little bit of understanding of the situation that this little boy was coming from, I scheduled an evaluation to determine where he was in his learning and development. Once again, I thought I was ahead of the game.

I will never forget the first time the caseworker invited me to meet him. During this visit, I would also be meeting with the birth parents.

When I arrived, we first met the parents, and then a little while after the little prince was brought in. I cannot put into words how I felt when I saw him. I instantly knew that he needed as much support as he could get. We sat in the room, getting to know each other. It was extremely uncomfortable, as we made small talk, and I tried to be open with the biological parents. We all did the best we could to make the visit seem pleasant and normal for the little boy. At one point, his bio-mom had a sucker, and when he saw it, of course, he wanted it. When he didn't get his way, he ran angrily at the door and began hitting his head on it. I had honestly never seen anything like this before. It was horrible! He was so upset. When the caseworker stopped him and picked him up, he arched his back and headbutted her. I was in total shock. He eventually calmed down, and everyone seemed to act as if this was normal. The rest of the visit went about the same way. Whenever he got upset, he hit his head, and eventually, someone calmed him down.

At the end of the visit, I talked to the caseworker and asked if this behavior was normal and asked why it was happening. She said his current foster parents had reported this behavior and that he had attachment issues. I wasn't sure how to feel, but I knew that this little boy needed my love and support.

After I got home, I kept thinking about the behavior I saw and also about how he looked. He just seemed different than any other little one I had been around. It was almost like he was in a shell. The case workers supported me throughout the process, but I also decided to look for outside resources. I contacted a children's therapy office and spoke with a therapist about his behavior. She told me to contact them as soon as I could pick him up and schedule an evaluation so we could get the supports we needed for him.

On our way home with him, I realized he needed us more than we could've ever known. He didn't seem to have joy, curiosity, or a desire to connect with me. I thought maybe this was because we were strangers. He was filled with so much rage and unhappiness that it was heartbreaking. I remember saying to my husband that I had never seen a child like him before. He didn't want to be held, he didn't play, and he rarely talked. I was at a loss as to how to help him.

The first few months are a blur because I worked so hard to show him that he was safe and trying to connect with him. Everything we did was a struggle and caused behavioral outbursts such as hitting his head, headbutting, yelling, and crying. I had a playpen that I tried to put him down to sleep in, but he repeatedly hit his head on the sides of it. Instead, I tried to snuggle him laying down, but he didn't want to, which ended in the same result.

Finally, I figured out that if I held him facing away from me on the sofa while rocking and repeating, "you are safe, it's okay to go to sleep," that he would eventually fall asleep. It was a long process of teaching and showing him that he was safe. We continued to try to get him to play and interact with us. It took a while, but one day we watched a kid's show on television, and it played the theme song, and I was dancing with him. He started to smile and even gave a little dance. It felt like we connected.

I threw myself into creating tools, reading books, and listening to podcasts in order to help this sweet little boy. I learned how to re-program his neurological system and taught him to trust me and feel safe. I watched him very closely because if something frustrated him, he would bang his head on the hardest thing closest to him. One of the things I did was create a "cozy area" and modeled for him how to say, "I am MAD," and showed him how to clench his fists and stomp his feet.

For eating, the strategy that worked best was teaching him how to dip his food, and we sang a "dip it" song that I learned from a Jillian Michael's podcast. To help with his communication, I took pictures of household objects, cut them out, and laminated them to teach him how to tell me what he needed. He showed us the picture or pointed to what he wanted or needed. When he pointed, we said the word that went with the picture. He caught on fast and started to look for the picture himself and eventually said the word. The more he was able to show or tell us what he wanted or needed; his frustration lowered. It was an amazing day when we no longer needed the envelopes.

His frustration seemed to be triggered mainly by being unable to do something, if he didn't want to do something, or when he thought his needs were not going to be met. The main goal was to be scheduled so he knew what to expect and to eliminate the struggle. One helpful tool was using a morning chart with pictures of everything that he needed to do each morning. They were laminated and had Velcro on the back. I made it fun for him to move them after doing each step. I also did the same with our nighttime schedule.

Even though we were making progress, I felt like a zombie, or like those memes you see online, a "mombie." That was me. I was exhausted, my body hurt, and I always tried to stay one step ahead of his rage. Finally, I had a meeting with the caseworker and the therapist, and they shared their concerns because they saw how exhausted and burned out I was getting. They got him into a daycare where he could be socialized with other kids, and I could get some much needed rest and time to practice self-care.

The daycare was amazing, and they supported us in using the tools we were trying. Since they had experience with so many children, they even had some suggestions that we tried. There were some big behavioral outbursts at daycare, but the positive thing was that he made lots of friends, and his teachers loved him. He was still hitting his head when he got upset. I remember once they called me because he had hit his head so hard on a window that he got sick.

Time went on, and soon it was time for him to start kindergarten. We were so blessed with his teacher, he made some great friends, and he had pretty much stopped hitting his head, but he began hitting and throwing things in class. In the classroom, he had a safe place to go when he got upset, and it seemed to work almost all the time.

Other times, he would run out of the classroom. He seemed to run to the same place, which was either the bathroom or the office. So we all figured if we knew where he was and if he was calming down, it was okay. As we got closer to the end of the year, he started to act out by running to the downstairs of the school, and one day he got mad and threw a pair of scissors. We made the tough decision to put him in a specialized program where they could better support him.

It's incredible to see how far my little boy has come. He is 100% ours now, as we adopted him. Unfortunately, once he was officially adopted, we lost our team. We were incredibly blessed to have case-workers and therapists that reassured me that I was making the right choices. All of that was gone. The last thing the therapist said to me was, "You know exactly what you are doing. This all comes naturally to you". She also encouraged me to share with other moms. She told me that she had all the faith in the world in my and my abilities. This made me think about how when you have a child. You're not given an instruction manual. The hospital hands you the baby and says congratulations, and then you're on your own.

I learned that it takes a village to raise a child, and so I've made it my mission to help overwhelmed moms let go of the struggle and find ease with my high-level support, strategies, and powerful tools to help them become the kind of mom they truly want to be.

Remember, mama, God has a plan, and you are meant to be the mom to your kids no matter how it came about. Even with that said, if you are struggling, it's okay to reach out for help. There are people that are there to support you.

**Michelle Den Boer**

"Nothing can dim the light that shines from within."

**MAYA ANGELOU**

EIGHT

## Finding Your Inner Power

YOU ARE THE SECRET SAUCE

For as long as I can remember, I've always been a talker. I remember as a child, lying in bed between my parents just talking and talking and talking, and my mom finally saying to me, *Shawna, you are talking too much. It's time to stop talking and go to bed.* I continued to hear this throughout my childhood. *Shawna is a lovely girl, but she talks too much!* As the years passed, I not only enjoyed talking to everyone, but I also loved to listen when people shared their stories, challenges, and triumphs. I found these stories fascinating, and most were very personal. It was common for people to come into my office, sit down, and start to tell me their stories while I was working. It took me many years, but I finally realized that listening to others was one of my strengths and that the more stories I heard, the more I wanted to help. Through the course of my career, I came to realize that I could use these talents to make a difference, an impact and take my business to the next level.

One particular memory that stands out for me was one day when I was having a conversation with a work colleague and he was telling me about a difficult customer. I mentioned that perhaps the customer had something going on in their life and asked my colleague if he had considered that fact. It appeared that he had not. I thought to myself, *wow – you just told me you don't care about your customers or their problems.* At that moment, my heart went out to all my customers. Two months later, this same colleague was let go from our company, and I knew that I was meant to apply for his position. I wanted something else. I wanted to make an impact. I wanted to help customers. I wanted to be out there in the world, talking to people and building relationships. Because I worked in a male-dominant industry, it was common to see a revolving door of male employees come and go from positions like this. Luckily, my experience growing up with three brothers helped me prepare for this type of environment.

My two older brothers and I are one year apart, and there are five years between my younger brother and me. I remember from a young age. I would always want to be doing whatever my brothers were doing. However, I was told no repeatedly because I was a girl. I often resisted stereotypical "girl" activities. I briefly partici-pated in ballet, tap, jazz, baton, an all-girl marching band, and figure skating, mostly to appease my mother. I eventually got into soccer and ringette, as I had already been playing goalie for my brothers to practice their slapshots while they'd cover me in pillows to soften the blows. My brothers and I had our ups and downs through the years, but I learned a lot from them, such as how to be strong, physically and mentally, I learned how to stand up for myself and speak my mind, I learned that no matter what status a man was labeled at work, that it was just a title. Once you remove the fancy title, he was a man, just like my father and brothers.

This served me well in a male-dominated industry. I would often think to myself. *I could do so much better than these guys. All they care about is making commissions. They are not interested in how we can help the customers, solve problems, or build relationships.* So, I decided to go for it and applied for the vacant position. I was excited and a little scared. I was excited as I knew I could do whatever I set my mind to, and a little scared at the same time because there were no women in that position in the company.

I still remember the feeling of shock running through my body when I was told that I was not being considered for the job. When I asked why the response was that a woman could not make more than her husband. My husband worked in sales with the same company, and there was a concern that I would be making more than him. I returned to my office shaking in anger. I remember the tears flowing as I closed my office door, sitting at my desk wondering what I should do next. I was 34 years old, and I would be damned if I was going to let a few men decide that I couldn't be in a sales position because I would make more money than my husband. Apparently, they didn't know me at all. I got up from my desk, held my head high, walked out of my office and into my husband's office, two doors down.

I walked into his office and shut the door behind me. He took one look at me, and panic came over his face. I told him that I was not being considered for the position, and he was shocked as well. He didn't care if I made more money than him. He was extremely supportive and told me I would be the best sales rep the company ever had.

My boss called me into his office later in the week, and his way of trying to soften the blow was by telling me that I was too good at my current job and that it would be hard to replace me. You see, he spent the summer months golfing with his buddies, who were also customers, and while he was out of the office most of the summer bragging about his golf game, I did his job. I responded to the emails, did his forecasts, managed the inventory, and so much more. It was all starting to make sense. Not only was I not a part of the old boys club, but I covered for him. He couldn't afford to lose me.

With all these emotions and feeling so taken advantage of, four weeks later, I handed in my resignation. I didn't even have another job lined up, all I knew was that I could do whatever I wanted, and I had the support of a loving husband. On my first day at home, I received a phone call offering me a consulting job. I was asked to oversee the setup, order the inventory, merchandising, marketing, and later manage the store front. I took the job on one condition, I would do all that was agreed upon, but I did not want to manage the store. I would, however, interview and hire a manager. On what I thought was the last day of my contract, the owner approached me and offered me a sales position. I didn't know exactly what the job was, but "sales" was in the title, so it was a big *heck yes* for me!

A couple of years into my sales career, I was at a conference in Nashville. After the conference ended, a group of us went out to a famous nightclub called Wildhorse Saloon. So, there I was sitting across from the VP of a billion-dollar company, and he asked me if I knew my worth? He said, "Shawna, as a young woman in a competitive male-dominated industry, you are either going to get beaten down or you are going to leave a mark. So, here is my advice to you, know without a doubt who you are, what you stand for, what you bring to the table as the value added, and most of all, know your own value – what you are worth, stand proud and firm." I remember that night like it was yesterday. I looked him in the eye, and with complete confidence, I said, "I know who I am, I know what I stand for and what I bring to the table, but let me ask you this, how does one know their worth?" He told me that to find out my worth, I was supposed to go out at least once a year and be interviewed by a competitor. When they gave me an offer, I was supposed to negotiate something better. He said to always have a scale in mind – top will be your shoot for the stars salary, the bottom where you are willing to start off, and the middle is your playing field. From that day on, I lived my career with that advice.

Knowing my worth was one of the wisest pieces of advice I was given. Several times in my 25-year career, I was close to leaving the industry to find something new, but I just kept getting pulled back in. I was even at the end of negotiations to buy an interior design franchise, ready to sign on the dotted line when I received a phone call from a distributor offering me a position. Interestingly enough, I looked down at the pen I was using at the time and realized that the pen I was holding had the same equipment brand name as the one I was being offered to represent. I took it as a sign from the universe.

What I didn't realize at the time, but I know now, is that life happens *for* you, not *to* you, and even though the next nine years were the most challenging and heart-breaking, they also brought the biggest lessons of my life. This particular phase of my career included the betrayal of a best friend, bullying by my boss, conflict with staff, jealousy, insecurities, lack of drive, lack of motivation, judging, blaming, shaming, endless drama, and so much negative energy. Going through all of that was stressful and traumatic. I was consumed with anger and periods of rage. The universe was sending me sign after sign to leave, telling me I was not meant to be working there.

In hindsight, I should have walked away after the first conversation about my raise. I was unhappy with the raise I was given, and so I booked a meeting with my boss to negotiate. I had my spreadsheet ready with the sales numbers before I started. I had the list of new accounts and monthly sales I brought in, which showed I had increased sales by two and a half times of the previous year, and I was only there six months. I presented the spreadsheet to the owner and ended up telling him that I would gladly leave and go with a competitor if he did not acknowledge my worth. In the end, I got the raise, even though working with this company was having hugely negative impacts on my health.

Despite all of this, I stayed. Four years later, however, I could barely get out of bed in the mornings and drag myself to work. I couldn't take it anymore. I was drinking way too much, and my friends and husband were worried about me. I became so angry. I was blaming everyone, and I was so deep in victim mode, I did not even recognize myself. Some days I would sit in my truck outside of the office crying, wondering what had happened. How and when did life get sucked out of me? Where did the positive, vibrant, confident woman go?

It all came crashing down in the summer of 2018. I began experiencing Benign Paroxysmal Positional Vertigo (BPPV), which are crystals in my inner ear, and when they become dislodged, they cause extreme vertigo. In addition, I was also experiencing extreme insomnia. As horrible as it was at the time, my doctor wanted me on modified duty, which meant no driving. I worked from home for a while, and then the company put me on leave.

During this time, I began to learn about mastering my emotions. I had been learning about mirrors, triggers, and limiting beliefs, learning about myself, about my power, and how I have given it away. I was also learning about forgiveness and how to move forward. Throughout all this transition, I was falling in love with the coaching industry, and I wanted to help others the way I had been helped.

The day my leave was over, and I was supposed to start back to work, I walked in and resigned. It was the most exhilarating day. Driving to the office, I had Alicia Keys, *This Girl is on Fire*, playing. I felt confident, strong, and grateful. I felt so much gratitude for the past nine years because I was able to look back with forgiveness, and I was able to let go and move on.

One day a dear friend introduced me to an online business opportunity, and I jumped on it. My confidence was back. I knew I could succeed at whatever I set my mind to. I just needed to be true to myself. Sixteen months later, the BPPV (Benign Paroxysmal Positional Vertigo) returned. There I was, laying in bed feeling completely helpless, stressed out, and disappointed in myself, and trying to be successful in an online business. This was not what I envisioned for myself. I was starting to feel the pressure, and this whole "online business" was feeling icky, slimy, and gross. I was feeling completely out of alignment and not true to my authentic self.

I knew something had to give. I decided to close the door of the online business, and I opened another. Walking through the new door ignited my soul on a whole new level. I dove deeper into emotional mastery. I felt alive when teaching and helping women. I loved helping women have *ah ha* moments, helping them feel confident and to thrive in their careers. As I was doing my inner work, I started to feel some resistance about putting myself out there and teaching the Emotional Mastery Program that I was trained for. I had to spend some time and reflect on why the resistance was present. It was in the quiet that everything became clear. I was comparing myself to others and trying to teach like them. I was successful because I refused to be programmed like everyone else. Yet here I was doing the very thing I disliked, to myself. It was time to get quiet again and ask myself, *Shawna, what do you want to do?*

I wanted to help women make money doing what they love. I wanted to help women feel confident about sales, for them to feel sexy and have fun. I wanted women to feel like Goddesses. I wanted women to know that selling can be as easy as having a conversation. I wanted women to see *selling* synonymous with *helping.* I wanted to bring sexy to sales. I wanted the women I worked with in sales to feel like a "Sexy Sales Goddess." With this new understanding and vision, the concept of Sexy Sales Goddess Transformation began. I remember feeling at peace, feeling like I was home again. The past 25-years of experience brought me to this point, where I knew I could make an impact on the world.

As I am putting the finishing touches on my course, I am feeling gratitude for my past experiences, joy, and excitement for what is yet to come, happiness in the present moment, knowing that I am creating my life every day. I have given myself permission to be unapologetically me. Writing this chapter has been very therapeutic.

I can see how my journey of success, burnout, disappointment, and then staying true to my authentic self can inspire and help others.

If you are unhappy and stuck like I was, know that there is *something* else out there for you. Don't just stay stuck because you have invested time, money, or relationships. Don't let fear, doubt, and uncertainty hold you back. It's time to get courageous, take a leap of faith, follow your heart, and do what makes you happy. All it takes is one step each day, moving forward towards your vision, desires, and dreams. Reach out for help. You are not alone. BELIEVE in yourself, and I believe in you!

**Shawna Roch**

"To free the voice is to free the person."

**KRISTIN LINKLATER**

NINE

# The Journey of Voice Awakening

## HOW FINDING YOUR VOICE CAN HEAL YOUR LIFE

I was eighteen and singing Debussy at a concert. It was the first time I had ever sung a solo in front of an audience. When the concert was over, I walked out of the building with my friend, still feeling a bit shaky and glad I had managed to do it. A couple of younger students were walking behind us. One of them asked, "Who was screeching so high?"

I froze. He was talking about me. No doubt about it.

That one remark cut so deep that I didn't sing in front of anyone else for another ten years. This was one of the traumatic experiences I have had of being silenced.

Much later, when I became a singing teacher, I was able to help hundreds of students who have had similar, painful experiences or who wanted to overcome their own inhibitions to speaking up or singing their hearts out. We work to heal their "voice story," where we look at how they have learned to speak, sing, communicate and express who they are from an early age.

Now, let me tell you my voice story – my journey to voice awakening.

I was born in Czechoslovakia in communist times; today, it's the Czech Republic. As a child, I was shy around grown-ups but very witty and fascinated by other children, nature, and the world. My mother tells me that I started speaking incredibly early and could say complete sentences by two years old, talking to everyone with ease. I also walked earlier than others. I just wanted to run after my cousin, who was six months older. I have often had challenges in my life that have made me grow really fast, but then resistance kicked in, and I would start doubting myself and hesitate to move forwards. Being a highly sensitive and empathic child, I picked up on any stressful vibrations around me, and there were many in my own family and in my environment.

When I was eight years old, our family of five came to Switzerland. We were political refugees after the Russian occupation of Czechoslovakia in 1968. We left everything behind to start a new life in a new country. It was challenging and sad to leave my grandparents behind, but as a child, I was also excited about all new.

Within a few days of arrival, I banged my fist onto the table and declared that from now on, my name was Dana, not Daja anymore. Daja was a name for babies! Somehow, I felt that my childhood was now over, and I was being called to grow up. My personality changed with my name, or rather, I changed my name because Daja did not fit my new role in life.

Did you know that your name is your first mantra? A mantra is words or syllables that hold a particular frequency and energy pattern that you evoke every time you speak it or hear it. Every time you change your name, it has a great impact on you. Your name is a bridge to your soul's sound signature. Later, I used this knowledge to help my students adjust their names or find a new one that better fits their life situation and inner feeling about themselves.

Back to my voice story. I picked up German and Swiss-German very fast. I needed German for the classroom and Swiss-German to survive in the playground. This made me the protector of my two little sisters, shouting at the neighbor boys who were bullying us for being foreigners. You know how children can be.

I could soon translate anything my parents needed to connect with our Swiss neighbors. This helped us assimilate more easily. I was the go-between, and I learned that communication holds extraordinary power.

Our capacity to communicate is what makes us human. The word communication comes from the Latin communicare, which means to share, inform. But you can also find common, shared by all and unity, being one. So, by communicating, we become one with each other.

My relationship with my mum was cordial and amicable, less so with my father. He held firm opinions of what is right and wrong, so I struggled to trust my own opinion, let alone speak it. There were many incidents where I would be silenced. For example, at the dinner table, he would be in his own mental world, inventing and solving problems, not being with us. We, three girls and mum, would chat away, and every so often, he would snarl at us and stop us from being talkative and sharing our stories. This was very hurtful. It spoiled our joy in expressing ourselves, and, truth be told, I believe that I still have some digestive problems stemming from that time.

What was strange was that my father was absolutely fine when we sang. Aah, how grateful I am for that today! We used to sing a lot while doing the dishes or while driving on holidays. He enjoyed the singing, but in any kind of intellectual discussion, he was the one who knew it all.

This explains why later, I was not timid in singing but utterly shy when speaking. This may seem astonishing, but it actually makes a lot of sense. Speaking is related to a person's mind and personality. Singing is deeply related to the soul, how we express it, and how we dare to show up in the world. Obviously, my father could relate to us on a soul level, but his personality needed to control what was said. Later I understood. He was carrying a story of survival that shaped his patterns for life. He had spent the Second World War as a tiny child hiding in sauerkraut barrels in a cellar, listening to the sounds of war above his head.

For my own survival, I chose to play the guitar and loved to sing along. Imagine sitting around a fire, songs and ballads of the 1960s and 1970s, Beatles' songs, and the like. In those days of the tape recorder, I would sit for hours alone in my room and record and transcribe the current hit songs and sing them out loud – unconsciously sensing that my dad must be hearing me. Oh yes, I adored my father and longed to be seen and heard. Are you with me on that?

Other than that, my life was pretty dry and weary. My high-level sensitivity led to feeling overwhelmed; I got psychosomatic ailments and had long stretches of depression. No one noticed me. I barely made it through the school system and the challenging times of adolescence.

It was my love for music and singing that pulled me through. I had a lovely voice, but no one ever mentioned that I should be a singer. I dreamed of becoming one, but no one ever knew since I was far too shy to speak about it. Some insensitive comments by classmates about my voice just cemented my keeping quiet. One boy said, "You speak like a farmer," and he mimicked the deep, hoarse voice you find in farmers in the Swiss Alps. I didn't know that girls' voices break too in puberty. That can make your voice sound odd at times, in my case, very deep. Usually, I sang very high and loud. I absolutely loved the vibrations of the sounds and the tingling sensations in my body.

The incident where I sang the solo at the concert was a severe shock and made me believe that I couldn't sing at all – since no one had ever really supported it anyway. Ooh, please, wait a minute – there was this ONE music teacher who had made me sing that solo piece!

He adored the timbre of my Slavic soprano voice. You can imagine why this compliment was very much subdued by the events that followed that performance.

In the following years, I hardly ever sang. Instead, I took to painting and doing handicrafts, which became my silent go-to creative expression. The burdens I carried and some disturbing events in the first few years after leaving my childhood home eventually led to a nervous breakdown. I was twenty-three years old but felt like ninety. My body had become completely stiff. I was having problems sleeping, eating, and digesting. My mind was utterly confused, and my heart was heavy. No voice, no future, no right to exist. Honestly, I was close to terminating my life. It's not easy to say this now – but these phases have come back again and again in my life.

Please be kind if you encounter someone who gives any such hints. I was so lucky to get proper support at this time. It took many years of therapy to heal and recover. First, there were the standard medical procedures, later I received holistic treatments, energy therapy, and spiritual counseling. I am forever grateful for those therapists and healers.

My main turning point came in a spiritual awakening at twenty-six years of age. Yes, it is often atrociously difficult times that culminate in a breakthrough. I'm sure we all know these times. In my case, it was a cataclysmic event – and from this point on, my voice would become my greatest healer. I was training to become a Polarity energy therapist. This was the energy therapy work that had helped me cure my body-soul disassociation and childhood traumas.

During one of the training sessions, we activated the throat chakra (chakra means "wheel" and refers to an energy vortex in your body). Suddenly, my throat chakra burst open. I released beautiful sounds through my voice and sensed myself flying across a turquoise sky with golds and blues intricately mingling. It was blissful beyond words. Later, others said that I sang like an angel.

Shortly after this life-changing event, my ability to sing overtones spontaneously appeared. This happened one day in class, as I started singing again. All of my chakras, the energy wheels along the spine, started turning one by one. My spine lit up with energy. People present said I was chanting overtones. I didn't even know what they were. It simply happened to me.

Overtone chanting is a technique that involves singing two notes simultaneously. It is also known as harmonics or throat singing and became popular in Europe in the late 1980s. Overtones create an otherworldly ambiance, conveying healing powers and activating higher states of consciousness. I became one of the highly accomplished female singers in Europe and shared this gift in many concerts and courses.

During this period, I developed spiritually with yoga and meditation, but my voice has proven to be my greatest healer! So, I followed the "journey of my voice," realigned with my soul, and awakened my true soul sound signature. This is how I express my inner being in this world.

I practiced and mastered multiple energy and healing techniques. I was able to heal and transform old pains and traumas and even past life blockages with the awesome power of subtle energies, sound therapy, and singing. Soon I started teaching others to do the same. These were exciting and creative years. I studied and performed varied singing styles. My favorites, though, are mantras and chants, overtones, and Shamanic journeys. I performed as a solo artist and in different ensembles, as well as with my own backing choir.

One of my significant milestones in the late 1990s was recording my CD "Ananda Khanda – Treasure of Bliss," featuring original mantra compositions and overtone chanting. Later, I also co-authored an award-winning book in German: "Simply Singing". I was overjoyed when I discovered the Indian music therapy called Sama Sonology. It literally connected singing, healing, and spiritual transformation. I shared my new skills in a holistic hospital, leading workshops and supporting students in their inner growth at my voice studio.

Finally, in the late 1990s, I was ready to heal my relationship with my speaking voice. I ventured into public speaking, presentation skills, acting, and voice coaching. I founded my company Voice Power and trained academics, business people, and leaders in voice awareness and presentation skills. Slowly my trust in speaking on stages grew, and I could finally speak up and share my knowledge outside of the familiar healing circles that I had been part of.

When at the end of the 1990s, the organizer of my singing and music therapy workshops asked me whether I wanted to run an educational course for their esoteric bookshop, I was deeply touched. I had gathered 12 years of experience in healing and voice work, but I was still hesitant.

By 2001, however, I had founded my sound healing school. In 36 weeks, I trained therapists, healers, and singers to use their voices to transform their energies, grow spiritually, and integrate their new sound and voice healing skills in their work. But then my life took a downward turn, again.

I was in a pattern of losing and finding my voice. Invariably, when hitting a roadblock, emotional or financial struggle, or losing a dear friend, I got disconnected from my inner self. Then I would shut down again and retreat completely. This pattern repeated itself, again and again. Nowadays, I know that these are essential times for inner growth. All seeds first need to germinate in the soil.

One great inner lockdown happened in my mid-forties after my long-term relationship came to a dramatic end. It was a huge life shock. I completely lost my voice - and my will and ability to sing. I still managed to teach somehow thanks to years of professional training, but the inner spark in my voice and my love of singing were blocked. I fled into the realms of intellect, overactivity, and trying to meet external demands. As a consequence, I was struggling to keep connected with my inner voice.

Then I started to feel unwell. It began with strong allergies and flu-like symptoms, and it took six months before the cause was discovered – histamine intolerance. My immune system became compromised, and I developed heart disease. Yes, now I finally understood. I had lost contact with my true heart.

Luckily, I was lovingly carried through this "dark night of the soul" by my spiritual teachers and friends – I'm ever so grateful for this grace in my life! I've got tears in my eyes writing this – I feel so much thankfulness. We are always held and protected, no matter what happens to us.

I was shown that I needed to reconnect to my soul's voice. In these life circumstances, this took patience and many years until I fully recovered. And guess what? Again, my voice became my healer. Slowly I started singing again and finding wondrous new ways to use my voice. This time, new mystical worlds opened up for me. I started singing different soul languages and all sorts of high-pitched frequencies called light language. My friends and clients would say that these sounds had tremendous healing power and impact on their consciousness. I was astonished by the effects and sensed a new awakening.

I took part in and guided spiritual journeys that helped me to unravel the newly found magic within myself. I discovered how I could use the sound of human voices to help people become aware of the subtle realms of nature. It can also be used to help anchor cosmic energies into Gaia, our beautiful mother Earth.

NOW, I am not holding back anymore and genuinely enjoy my self-expression. I happily share my voice and teach others to discover their authentic voice, to speak up, or sing. I feel called by my inner voice to do healing on the planetary and collective human level. I have started teaching internationally and am taking my Awakened Voice Academy to the next level.

My message to you, dear reader, is this:

No matter how often you get shut up by someone in your life, no matter how many dramatic circumstances are thrown at you, no matter how many times you need to go quiet to survive – know that you can always realign with your inner voice, allow the flow of creative sound energies to clear all blocks and hesitation - and express yourself to the world with joy.

Whether you speak, chant or sing, I invite you to share your awakened voice, your truth and wisdom, and your beautiful heart with the world.

**DanaGita Stratil**

"Start over, my darling. Be brave enough to find  the life you want and courageous enough to chase it. Then start over  and love yourself the way you were always meant to."

**MADALYN BECK**

# TEN

## I'll Never Be Like Them

### CHOOSING MY OWN FUTURE DESPITE MY PAST

I was five years old when I had my first clear memory of the fear and anger that was always in our house. I was hiding in the very back corner of my family's garage one afternoon. It was pitch black; the lights were out. As I sat among the boxes and the junk, still just a little girl hiding in the dark, I remember saying to myself over and over again, "I will never be like them. I will never be like them. I will never be like them".

I was referring to my Mom and Dad. I don't remember what had happened or why I was hiding in the garage, but it was a defining moment in my life. I never was like them, and for years when there was no one to help guide me, I would think back to the promise I made to myself. I would think of what they would do and then do the opposite, and it did help guide me for years.

Now, as an adult, when I look back at that little girl, it makes me sad to think that she was less scared in a dark garage, all by herself, than in her own home.

The stories that follow certainly aren't all that happened but will hopefully give you a good representation of what it was like.

I had a challenging life growing up. It was filled with anger, fear, verbal and emotional abuse, and neglect. There was continual loud fighting, and it was nasty as both of my parents were alcoholics. Dad would often live and work in a different city, but he wasn't around much even when he did live with us. The fighting was the worst when Dad was there; however, Mom's focus was on me when he was gone. Perhaps because I was the youngest and easiest target, or maybe Mom had other reasons. I don't know, and I suppose it doesn't matter, as the outcome was the same regardless.

When you'd first meet my Mom, she would seem alright, but it didn't take long to see things were a bit off. Everything was about her, with zero regards for what it may do to others, especially me. There was never any remorse, empathy, or regret, and she wouldn't have hesitated to make the same decision again.

I have a brother that is five years older. He was around when I was little, but I didn't see him for years once he was old enough to move out.

As a child, I was incredibly shy. I'm sure that moving all the time and continually being the "new kid" didn't help. At a young age, I learned to stay quiet at home to avoid becoming the target. Keep out of sight, out of mind, and never show weakness was the easiest way to make it through each day.

Money was always tight, and not knowing where your next meal was coming from was a daily worry. We continually moved; I can count six cities and one of those cities three different times, with about 30 houses and 11 schools. I don't know why we moved so much, but I do know it created instability and uncertainty in my life.

I was born in Kelowna, BC, Canada. It's a beautiful city with hot summers and resides on a massive lake. We moved from Kelowna when I was three months old to Bellingham, Washington, in the US, where my Dad was already living and working.

We were in Bellingham for 12 years and lived in four houses. The time we were there felt like it got worse, or maybe I was just getting older and started to realize. There are a few times in Bellingham that stick out to me. The first was that little girl in the garage starting to learn how to hide. The second was a year or so later, and another house.

I woke up one afternoon on the couch with Mom, Dad, and my brother standing nearby talking. Mom's arm was in a sling, and my brother's leg was wrapped up. Mom, my brother, and I had been in a car accident the day before. I don't remember the accident or three days prior as I had banged my head and probably had a concussion. Mom and my brother went to the hospital; I was taken home to sleep on the couch for the next day and a half. We lived in the States without medical, and the decision to save on the bill by taking me home was made. The decision wasn't a surprise; it was the way it was.

One more move in Bellingham; I was 11 and with money being tighter than it had ever been, still staying safe was always my main focus. Dad wasn't around much, but Mom was, and she certainly didn't hide what she felt about me. There were many times that the phone was cut off, and having food was something that was always on my mind. That being said, those issues were easy compared to the days ahead. There was a massive tank under the front yard with oil to run the furnace, and we ran out. Dad was living in Vancouver, BC, at the time, and there was no money to buy more oil. That meant no heat or hot water for a few weeks in the middle of a cold, damp winter in Northern Washington State. To stay warm, I'd sleep in every piece of clothing I owned. When I needed to bathe, I'd boil as much water as possible, trying to keep it warm until I had accumulated enough for a bit of a bath.

No heat was truly horrible but not knowing if you would have anything for your next meal was worse. It was here where I learned to stop eating even when I was still hungry to try and save it for the next day. "I might be more hungry tomorrow than I am today," I would think. It's a lesson that I wouldn't want anyone to learn. It's also a hard lesson to unlearn.

Time to move again. This time my Mom, brother, and I left Bellingham in the middle of the night. I'm not sure why we had to sneak away; all I knew was we needed to keep it quiet.

I wasn't allowed to tell anyone we were leaving or even say goodbye to my friends. The three of us crossed the border and came back to Canada. We showed up in Kelowna at my Grandma's, my Mom's Moms, home. She had a tiny little wartime house and took the three of us in. All we had brought was one suitcase to share between us.

We didn't live there long, but the memories are not good. A friend I made came over one afternoon, and Mom was going to walk into town with us. Once my friend arrived, Mom let me know she did not like what I was wearing. She insisted I go inside to change when I came back out wearing the same clothes; she was not happy. I didn't have anything else; the few clothes I had were all in the laundry. Mom made it clear she didn't want to be seen with me and wouldn't let me walk with her and my friend to town. I watched Mom talk and laugh with my friend while I walked behind.

Grandma's neighborhood had gone downhill over the years, and late one night, I heard a lot of noise. Looking out the front room window, I saw the man and woman that lived across the street fighting. They were in the front yard; she had just run from inside, and he was hitting her. I'm sure she had come out to get help, but help isn't what she got. She got a bunch of neighbors gathered on the street watching.

I grabbed the phone to call the police, but Mom, now angry with me, hung the phone up, telling me it was none of our business. It was one more time I promised myself, "I will never be like them." There was nothing I could do to help that poor woman. I pray she was able to get help, not only for that night but for her future. At 12 years old, I had already seen more than anyone should.

About six months after arriving at Grandma's, it was time to move again. This move was to Prince George, a reasonably large logging town in the middle of the province. Dad was with us this time, and Grandma came as well. She sold her house that she and Grandpa Jim had worked so hard to pay for before he passed away. The money was then deposited into Grandma's bank account.

Prince George is where things went from bad to worse for me with Mom. The first place we lived in was a big apartment block on the 4th or 5th floor. Dad was out of town, and the fire alarm went off in the middle of the night. Being an incredibly sound sleeper, it took me a while to wake up, but when I did, I was alone. No one was in our apartment. I looked outside, and I could see uniforms, flashing lights, and people all over the street waiting for the firemen to clear the building. I was scared; it was so loud, and the building was dark. I didn't know what to do, so I stayed in the apartment.

The following day, I asked Mom why she didn't wake me up. She said she figured it was probably a false alarm. Thankfully it was, or perhaps I wouldn't be here today. That was the first time I realized that Mom not only ignored me but was willing to actually put me in harm's way. It was the first but not the last.

Another new house in Prince George and the fighting continued to get worse. One day I got what I thought was my regular period again, but it wasn't a period. It lasted for about three weeks and was heavier than any period should ever be. I started to get weaker and weaker to the point where I couldn't walk more than 10 feet without sitting down. Thin, pale, and going through boxes of expensive pads could not have gone unnoticed—we barely had the money for food! Mom still hadn't taken me to the doctor, even with medical care being free in Canada, so that wasn't a factor. Dad began accusing me of using drugs, believing that must have been the reason I was so tired. I told him the truth; I didn't do drugs, "those kids" scared me! He didn't believe me. It was summertime, and I was on two months break from school. That meant no one around to notice what was going on and no one to help me.

My best friend in Prince George was Christine, and she came over one day. We were young, but she must have realized just how serious the situation was and told her Mom. I inferred this because Mom took me to the doctor that day, which I'm sure she wouldn't have done unless forced. From the doctor's, I was sent straight to the hospital to be admitted. Once I was in my hospital room, I heard the doctor say to the nurse. "She was a day, to a day and a half away from cardiac arrest. She should be taken away."

I wasn't taken away, and to my knowledge, it was never looked into. My blood was so low that my veins had collapsed, and I coded while beginning a blood transfusion. The girl I was sharing the room with described how I had started to convulse when a code blue was called, bringing everybody running. I guess it won't surprise you that I still hate needles.

The girl I shared the hospital room with and I were the oldest in the unit. A few times, when all the little kids were asleep, the nurses would let us have wheelchair races down the halls. I love that memory, and I hope the nurses knew how much that meant to me.

Because of my age, the doctors spoke to Mom about my medical condition and why it all happened. I asked Mom at the time what happened, but she couldn't remember what the doctors said. I wish I would have overheard their conversation because I still don't know what the cause was.

Life up until this point was very dark and cold; however, the years I was heading into were the hardest. I honestly didn't know how I would survive, and at times, I wasn't sure if I wanted to. That thought terrified me. At this time, I would start to see an image of nothing but a dark grey sky with a circle in the distance, as you would see at the far end of a tunnel. The circle was full of sunlight, and I could feel the warmth and happiness. I clung to it with all my might; somehow, I knew it was my future. Once I was away from Mom, the fighting and the abuse. I would desperately cling to the hope of this future. On the days when things were nasty, my hands would ball up into fists, and I would say over and over again,"You are not taking that away from me!"

It was what kept me going; I needed to hold on. Mom could not take away my future, one that wasn't cold, dark, and full of pain, as long as I just—hung—on. It was all I had, and I'd cling to that in the years that followed.

We were about to make another move. I was now 13, and Christine's Mom offered to let me live with them. I told my Mom that I could stay behind. Mom thought long and hard about leaving me, but in the end, she said no. I knew she wanted to, but she was still in contact with Aunts and Uncles that would have noticed I was gone and asked questions.

This move was to a small logging town even further north in BC called Terrace. It was pretty, in the middle of nowhere and cold. I went to two schools in Terrace and made some friends, especially one named Jamie. Our lockers were next to each other when we were 13. I'm 51 now, and I still consider him one of my best friends.

Mom and Dad's fighting continued to get even worse, Grandma still lived with us, and by this time, my brother had moved to Alberta, Canada. I was fourteen and working after school and on weekends to help pay for anything that I needed. One day, I came home from school, and Dad said he'd give me a ride to work which he never did, so I knew something was up.

We stopped for a pop across the street from the mall. We didn't stay long, but as I was about to leave, Dad told me he was moving out and wouldn't be there when I got home. I walked over to work a little stunned but when I got home is when it was truly horrible.

Grandma was in the living room bawling. Mom had just told Grandma that all of her life savings, all the money left from the sale of her little house, were gone. Mom said that it was Dad who had spent it.

I suspect that Dad may have spent some of the money, but Mom had Power of Attorney. Only Mom had access to the money, and, in all likelihood, it was probably Mom who would have taken and spent her own mother's savings.

With Dad now moved out, there was no doubt that Mom wouldn't support us. By this time, I was fifteen, and with all the moving, I wasn't doing very well in school. So, I quit, got a full-time job right away at a bookstore, and shortly after that, I was promoted to assistant manager. One day, out-of-the-blue, Mom took Grandma and me from Terrace to Kelowna, a fourteen-hour bus ride. I didn't know why we were going, and neither did Grandma. The first day in Kelowna, we arrived at a nursing home, and Mom told Grandma that we were leaving her there, that it was going to be her new home. Grandma was in shock, and when I went to hug her goodbye, she clung to me, begging me not to leave her there. I was still a child; I felt so helpless.

Grandma's money was gone. Her daughter left her without notice in a nursing home where she would live for the next 18 years, and there was nothing Grandma could do about it. I never saw one bit of remorse or empathy from Mom.

Mom and I headed back to Terrace, and a few months later, she announced to me, "I'm moving to Kelowna, and you can't come with me. You have three weeks to find somewhere to live," she said. I was only fifteen and cannot even describe the terror and debilitating fear I felt. I was being left alone, without a home and nowhere to go.

The time was going fast. The three weeks were almost up. I still had no place to live, and I knew Mom was going whether I had a place to live or not. I was desperate and had asked everyone I knew if I could live with them, but I had found nothing. Dad still lived in Terrace; I didn't know where he lived or his phone number. Dad stopped by my work about a week before Mom was leaving, and we went for pop. I told him in a few days; I was going to be homeless.

"I'm going to be living in the ditch soon." I was genuinely terrified. He laughed, thinking it was a joke, but it wasn't. I got up, left, and headed back to work when Dad caught up and stopped me. "You can stay at my place for one night. But my first priority is to my girlfriend." All I could think was, "What is one night going to do." I had been looking for three weeks. I hadn't expected him to take me in; I was just hoping for some help.

Three days before Mom was leaving, I finally met a girl who said I could move in with her. She was 21 and said she'd make room. The day Mom left, she called a cab to take her to the Greyhound Station. On the way, Mom dropped me off in front of my friend's house so my friend could show me where I would be living. I got out, grabbed my suitcase, and the cab drove away. I don't think Mom even got out to say goodbye. I was scared. I hadn't even seen the basement suite and had only met my new roommate the one time. I remember pulling my little suitcase behind me, filled with everything I now owned.

It would be thirty years before I could even think about that night. I would become completely overwhelmed with fear and pain whenever I tried. Mom didn't just leave me. She waited as long as possible to give me notice, then watched me struggle to find a home, all the while ignoring me. Mom then put everything we owned into storage, leaving me with only a few pieces of clothing. Mom had made my situation as hard as possible while setting me up for failure.

I lived in that suite for a couple of years, working at the bookstore and going to the bar way more than I should have, especially since I was still underage. Those couple of years were hard and the only time in my life that I didn't have any friends. The kids I had gone to school with were still in high school doing what kids should be doing at that age. My life was very different from theirs; I lived on my own, trying to figure out how to survive. Then there were the 20-year-olds that I knew from working, but I was still only 15 and didn't fit in with them either. It was a terrifying, lonely time. I always knew I was only one wrong decision away from ending up homeless, and no one would have come looking for me.

I woke up one morning and knew I needed to get out of Terrace. I was seventeen and responsible, but I was going down the wrong path. Without a second thought or a plan, I went to work and gave them my two weeks' notice. I then walked across the mall to where Jamie worked and gave him the news. That night I called my Mom told her I was moving down to Kelowna and staying with her.

I always tried to give Mom the benefit of the doubt. I thought for years there must have been a reason Mom couldn't take me to Kelowna with her. Little by little, I had to face the truth. There was no one around; Mom didn't have to worry about what people would think of her if they knew she left me. There was no one to notice I was gone.

Mom had planned it all out, right down to leaving me behind. Mom told Grandma about the money being gone once she had secured a room in the nursing home for Grandma, and that takes time. Mom next found herself a place in Kelowna and gave her notice for the apartment in Terrace. It was only then, when everything was set, she finally told me she was leaving.

Mom had it planned out, right down to leaving me behind. Mom had no intentions of ever seeing me again after she left me in Terrace. I didn't realize, or more likely, I couldn't face the truth. What I did know was I needed a connection to someone in this world. How could I survive not being connected to anyone—even if it was a bad connection?

I showed up in Kelowna to stay with Mom. Looking back now, I'm sure she was not happy about that. I didn't know that she was living in a motel, how long she had been there, or where else she had lived. I stayed in the motel with Mom for about a month or so, just long enough for me to get a job, receive my first paycheque, and put a damage deposit on an apartment for her. That was the start of the next twelve years, where I would pay for many of my Mom's expenses while also supporting myself.

I thought I continued to support Mom because I didn't want to do what she had done to me. She had just left regardless of what would happen to me; I will never be like her, I would think. However, years later, I would realize that there was more to it. The abuse and neglect I endured were still taking their toll on me. I felt I owed her.

I had my place; I found a better job, and I had wonderful friends. Life was better than before; I was always living on the edge when it came to Mom. When was the next urgent call for more money going to come; it was never-ending. The better I was doing financially, the more money Mom seemed to need. I could never put some aside for emergencies, and the stress was taking its toll. I had to start facing the fact that she's using me and always had been. That hurt too much to admit to myself.

One day after work, I stopped by Mom's to see how she was doing, and out of nowhere, she turned to me and said, "I always thought you'd end up on the streets." She was referring to leaving me in Terrace by myself at fifteen. She thought I'd end up on the streets, and she left anyway. She still left! Telling me years later what she had thought was only to hurt me, and it did.

I was now in my late twenties, and the friends I had were hard-working, intelligent, and funny. They cared about people to and they cared about me. I knew a few were Christians, and at first, that just didn't make sense to me. They were good people, and they were also Christians. Mom had always told me to watch out for "those people." It was one of the few times Mom ever gave me advice, and she was wrong. I very slowly started to take an interest in God. I thought I'd see what church was all about. It took me a few years to let my guard down, but eventually, I became a Christian. I started to realize that although I hadn't known God, God had always known me; he had been there protecting and guiding me. There are far too many times to share here.

The years with Mom were more than I could take. It got to the point where I knew I needed to leave Kelowna. I needed to distance myself from her. She was using me and making me feel incredibly horrible about myself, just like I did growing up. It was about this time that a business associate of mine came up to Kelowna from Abbotsford, BC, just outside Vancouver. He asked me if I was seeing anyone and said he had a guy he'd like me to meet. I laughed and said no, I wasn't dating anyone, and no, I wasn't interested in a blind date. Well, that didn't last long. Eventually, we started talking on the phone; his name was Paul. Our several-hours-long phone conversations turned into a long-distance relationship, which meant back-and-forth road trips between Kelowna, where I was living, and three hours away to where Paul was.

Before I knew it, I was offered a job with a company Paul was working with, and I took it. I thought I'd give it a try. I had nothing to lose; if it didn't work, I'd decide what to do then. I knew for sure I needed a change. I needed to move away from Mom, and I knew I needed to see where it was going with Paul.

That was twenty-one years ago. Paul and I are married, bought a house, and have two beautiful boys. We still live in the same house they were born in. Paul also became a Christian shortly after our first son was born.

Although the years after leaving Kelowna were good with Paul and our two boys, it didn't get easier with Mom. I tried to keep in touch with her, but it was a challenge as Mom never called me. The one and only time she did call was the day before Paul and I were getting married, and that was to tell me she wasn't coming. I wasn't surprised, but none the less it still hurt, and it meant that I had no family at our wedding. Dad hadn't been around for years, and my brother didn't even respond to the invitation. Paul's parents were here from England, and we had our wonderful friends; it was beautiful, but that little piece of me still hurt.

Life went on, and we had our first son. We were building our life here when I started to have health problems. Eventually, Paul and I would drive out to UBC, a university in Vancouver, where I was diagnosed with MS. It was a quiet drive home when I suddenly realized we might be pregnant with our second child. The look of shock on Paul's face when I said that was quite funny. The next day we took a pregnancy test, and yes, we were pregnant. It was a lot to handle in two days: MS one day and pregnant the next. At least we had something wonderful and exciting to share. I would tell friends first about the MS, they never knew what to say, but then I could tell them we were pregnant and end on a happy note.

I waited a few weeks to phone Mom as she had a way of making good things bad and bad things worse. I started with the news about the MS, but before I could tell her I was pregnant, Mom said she had to go and hung up the phone. The news wasn't about her, and she didn't want to deal with it. I didn't speak to Mom again for a few years. I went through pregnancy, labor, and the first year and a half of raising our second son, and Mom still didn't even know I had been pregnant. We finally did send Mom a birth announcement when our son was a year and a half old. I always worried when we went to Kelowna to visit friends that we'd run into Mom without her even knowing we had another son. Mom didn't respond, again, not a surprise.

My Dad had started to reach out to me after not speaking for about eighteen years, and we discussed perhaps having a visit. Around the same time, our oldest son, five years old now, started continually asking about his Grandparents and wanted to meet them. I always thought the boys had a right, but I would be incredibly protective. Paul and I decided we would take the boys to meet their Grandparents. We headed for Kelowna, 3 hours away, to spend a few hours with Mom, then we'd drive another hour to see my Dad and his wife.

When we arrived at Mom's, she met her two grandchildren. Mom never asked anything about them, barely even looked at them. She talked about some far-fetched health issues she was having, as she had done for years. When it was time to go, we were standing outside her apartment door to say goodbye when she basically shut the door in our faces. That was the last time I ever spoke to my Mom, and our oldest son never once asked about her again.

We then drove the hour to my Dad's for a visit. It was the first time my husband and sons had ever met Dad, and I wasn't sure what to expect. Over the next year, we built a bit of a relationship. Dad was then diagnosed with cancer, and it moved quickly. I started making day trips to visit, and near the end, I was making a few day trips a week. I would drop the boys off at school, drive a couple of hours, spend time with Dad and his wife before I would start heading home in the late afternoon.

The day Dad passed away, I was visiting him in palliative care. He was weak and could barely talk. The last thing he was able to say to me was, "I'm sorry." I'll never know what he was sorry for, but it didn't matter. I had already forgiven him years earlier. Dad's wife wanted to spend his final moments with just the two of them. I started the drive home, and when I pulled into our driveway, I looked at the time in the car. It was 5:04 pm. A few hours later, we received a call from my Dad's wife telling us he had passed away at 5:04 pm. That was ten years ago.

Although my brother and I haven't spoken in years, his wife has Paul's number for emergencies. Seven months ago, Paul got a phone call from her to tell us Mom had passed away. Sometime in the previous 14 years, my Mom had moved to Alberta, Canada, where my brother lives. I don't know when she moved; Mom never told me she was moving or even a contact number. In case I wasn't sure if she wanted to keep in touch or not, that was a sure sign she did not.

I had tried to prepare myself for the day I'd find out Mom had passed. Although I wasn't sure what I'd feel, I knew it wouldn't be grief. I wasn't prepared for what did end up happening. I knew my childhood was horrible and abusive. As an adult, I thought I had already dealt with the past. I'm in a good place now; I'm safe and have been for years. I read years ago that when you're in a truly safe place, everything that you haven't dealt with you now will need to. Before Mom's passing, she was old; she was weak and lived in a nursing home. I didn't know I couldn't truly feel safe until she was gone. The pain and fear I felt each day as a child were more than I could handle at that time. I had been in continual survival mode, continual flight or fight. My emotions were still muted, still trying to protect me, not letting me feel what it had indeed been like. Now there was no need for that protection anymore; those muted feelings no longer needed to be muted.

Perhaps the best way I can explain it is like this. It is as though you're watching an intense movie. You feel sad and might cry or be scared for the people, but you know it's just a movie, and you know it'll end. Suddenly you realize it wasn't a movie, and you weren't watching from a distance. Everything you just witnessed was you; it was actually all about you. Suddenly 51 years of emotions hit me and struck me hard. Everything I couldn't face at the time because it would have been more than I could handle came at me full force. I didn't see this coming, and it hasn't been easy. I still have work to do, but I'm glad that this has happened. I feel emotionally healthier, and I have become a softer person already. The wall I had put up to protect myself was also blocking the people I love from genuinely getting close.

The fragments of my life have started to make sense, and I'm able to put the pieces together. I have worked hard over the years to not only survive but to thrive, and this is one more step in my journey.

The road from my childhood has been long and hard. It's taken time, guts, and courage to face how I saw myself and the world around me. In my twenties, I would look at each of my thoughts and ask myself, "Is that how I truly feel, or is that something I need to leave behind." It gave me the chance to leave everything I was told where it belongs and find out who I truly am.

I'm here with my family, my friends, and my God in a life so different from what I ever thought possible. Paul and I have had some challenges - every couple does - but we made a commitment 21 years ago and are stronger now than we started. We have two incredible boys, 18 and 15 years old. They're both intelligent, kind, fun, and good people.

I've been there while they've grown up, and I can't believe what a true blessing it has been. If there is anything that I would hope people could take away from my story, it is this.

The first is where you come from does not determine who you are. Don't allow what has happened in your life to define you. When I was growing up, I had no control over what happened to me. I didn't cause it, and I couldn't have stopped it. How my life was, as a child, was controlled by my parents. How my life is, as an adult, is controlled by me. My decisions and my attitude determine how my life will be.

The second is forgiveness. Forgiveness is hard; it takes time and work to get there. It's not always a quick process, and you may need to return to it numerous times, but I don't believe you can truly move on without it. We can't carry our anger with us if we want to have a happy and fulfilled life. When you hear that forgiveness is all about the one doing the forgiving, it's true. My Mom had no remorse over anything that happened and didn't feel that she had done anything that needed forgiveness. Forgiving my Mom and Dad has freed me to live a life full of love, happiness.

For women who've lived through abuse, the damage it has done can still live in the shadows. Take the steps to shine a light on them. See them for what they are, the lies your mind and body still haven't abandoned.

For those of us walking beside her, take her hand, let her know you're there.

**Kelly Cross**

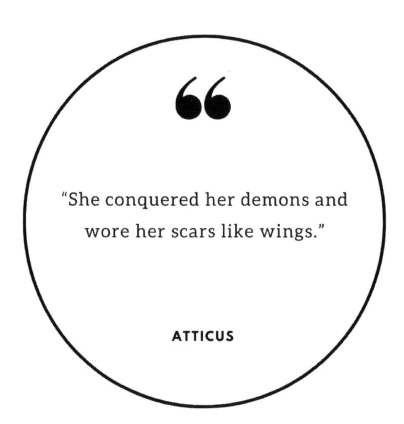

"She conquered her demons and wore her scars like wings."

ATTICUS

# ELEVEN

## Abandoned

### ONE RESPONSE TO FEELING ABANDONED IS TO ABANDON YOURSELF

I had a dream life. Married to a good guy, an amazing kid, owned my own house, budding career, even has the fluffy dog to go with it. I worked hard for almost ten years to be at a point in my life where I didn't have to worry if I could buy groceries that week or not. Just like that, it was all gone - in the blink of an eye.

In August 2016, my world came to a stop when my father-in-law passed away from a long battle with cancer. That day was the day my husband changed forever. I always say that two men died that day: my father-in-law and the man I married.

My husband was consumed by grief, went into a dark hole, and I never saw him again. I tried to be a good supportive wife. I researched, learned, and fought for two years. Even to the point, I found out that animals help with depression and grief, so I drove to Montana (11.5 hours away) to adopt a dog, but it wasn't enough - I couldn't get him back. He was done with the marriage, and in June of 2018, he left.

I was LOST. I felt abandoned. All my stability walked out the door. That budding career of mine, well, it's commission based. Not the most stable income. When it's good, it's good when it's bad, well, I am foraging for berries in the forest so I can eat (not actually, but I am trying to paint a picture here). My rock was gone; the one person who could help me through my anxiety was no longer there. This is the beginning of what I like to call my dark days.

We all have those days that we would like to forget well, let me tell you I have a whole year. What's that you say? Of course, you want to forget the year your husband left you. I mean, who wouldn't. The fact of the matter is that the marriage ending was amicable. I truly wanted him to be happy. If it wasn't with me, then so be it.

Shortly after me and my husband split. I decided I wanted to avoid my pain instead of going through it and decided to date, and this is the start of the real story. I met a man who seemingly adored me. He said and did all the right things, but there was one problem, he was married. He told me how he wanted to ride off into the sunset together. Promises of building a life together and all the other bull shit lies a man in his position would tell you. I stayed with him for almost a year. He was a mentally abusive narcissist. He would constantly accuse me of cheating. He would often go through my phone to "check it". I couldn't even shave my legs without there being a fight because he said that "I was looking to go out on the town and slut it up". He threatened if I told his wife or if any of my friends got any ideas, he would burn down my house - because he would have nothing left.

My mental health deteriorated even more to the point where I was so cruel and mean to my stepmom one night, who has shown me nothing but love for years, I almost lost her and my dad forever (to this day, I carry the most shame about that). Why did this outburst happen? Because the man I loved was on vacation with his wife.

After that I went to the doctor to get medication, he was all for this I might mention. Why? Because I was so numb I didn't care about anything anymore. My business suffered. I couldn't afford to pay my mortgage anymore, and yet another person had to come to my rescue. For six months, my sister paid so I could just have a roof over my head.

You would think this would knock some sense into me, but it didn't. Why might you ask? Well, because I didn't want to live. The thing I feared most being on my own, alone and abandoned.

The funny thing was that I was being abandoned. Every. Single. Day. He would leave me to be at home with his wife. I was repeating and reliving the moment my husband left me every single day. The one thing I fear most I had manifested, and I was still blind to it all. No matter how many times people told me to leave, I didn't listen. I am a Taurus. After all, we are notoriously stubborn.

I eventually came to my senses and made a choice. With help and guidance from my counselor, I was able to walk away. She showed me that if I didn't break this cycle, then it was never going to end, and I would remain being broke and broken.

A few months went by, and I thought I was done processing and ready to move forward with my life. That was a lie. I started dating another abusive man who assaulted me. When it happened, I was so broken and lacked so much self-love that I didn't even recognize it as rape.

I felt like I was to blame too. All I knew was I didn't like that this had happened. I started to distance myself from him and made sure to never be alone with him again. I started to notice that I was having changes down there. If you get my drift, I asked the rapist if I had anything to worry about, and his response was, "Do you? You're the one dating". I hadn't seen, talked to, or looked at another man since the night he raped me. I went to the doctor for my regular check-up and told him what happened. He gave me a full STI panel. On New Years' Eve 2019, I found out that I contracted chlamydia.

When I found out, I was thankfully with my best friend Anthony. He comforted me as I cried because I felt like I was dirty and unlovable. Anthony told me that it wasn't my fault and that my attacker didn't listen to me saying no and this was the result. You should charge him with assault. I just wanted to move past it, and I didn't want the guy anywhere near me. At that moment, Anthony said to me, "If he ever comes near you again, I will be having a conversation with him with my boot on his neck". I want to clarify that never happened. Anthony is the most kind-hearted, gentle person you could meet. But in that moment I realized that this wasn't alright. How upset he was showed me that what happened was, in fact, assault.

That was the moment that I vowed to heal my wounds before someone other than myself got hurt. My daughter deserved a mother that was healthy and whole. Who was able to take care of herself and her child.

I worked hard to build myself up. Some days were hard, and I didn't want to get out of bed. I wanted to hide from the world because I didn't know where my place in it was. Then I would look into my sweet little girl's eyes, and I knew. If I couldn't show up for myself, then I had to show up for her because she deserves the world. She should not suffer because of my choices. That's what got me through.

I knew being a mother was a gift, but I never really understood it until then. She saved me - when I couldn't save myself.

Now I wake up every morning excited for what the day brings. I still have shitty days, but they don't make me curl up into a ball and hide from the world. I learned my worth. I can say now I truly love myself more than I ever have! I am a badass person!

Life will throw you around; it will try to break you. Hell knows that it did break me, but I was so fortunate to have people in the ring with me fighting for me when I couldn't. I am thankful for each and everyone one of them. To my sister for keeping the roof over my head, to my stepmom for your forgiveness, my friends for your unwavering support - you let me cry on your living room floor, took me to the doctor to get meds, called me to check-in, dragged me out of the house. I can't thank you enough.

Mostly thank you to my blue-eyed baby girl who didn't even know what she did - she saved me.

My final message is this :

It is ok to feel your pain and rely on others in your inner circle. They will be there for you if you just ask. Find your purpose and keep going. And if you don't have any love for yourself, just know - I love you.

**Marie**

"Mirrors are just glass and you are more than that."

HEALTHYPLACE.COM

## TWELVE

## How My Mirror Saved My Life

### MY BATTLE WITH ANOREXIA

I was 29 years old when I first noticed I had a problem. It was the year 2000, and I was on stress leave from work, feeling stressed and drained. I knew something was wrong. I lacked energy, and all I wanted to do was sleep, but one morning I dragged myself out of bed and decided to have a shower. With my towel wrapped around me, I walked into my room. As my towel dropped, I caught a glimpse of myself in the mirror. It was like a light bulb turned on. Who the hell was that person in the mirror? It sure wasn't me, or at least not the real me. All I saw was a skeleton. My face was hollow, and my arms and legs were like sticks. I stared at the stranger in the mirror, and I was horrified. My rib cage rippled through my skin. I had no meat on my bones at all. I was a little, scrawny person. I knew I wasn't in a good situation, and I knew it was all my fault.

For about a week, the image I saw in the mirror stayed in my head. I caught myself looking in the windows of stores I passed by, in my windows at home, and even in the car windows parked on the road. Everywhere I looked, that skeleton was there. I started to feel something awkward inside. I knew I needed to see a doctor, but I didn't even know how to approach the subject. What would I say? I felt like a chicken wing. I knew something had to be done, so I decided to save myself. This is the day I chose to change my life.

I sat in the doctor's office, waiting for my name to be called. I was so confused. How was I going to explain to the doctor that I needed help because I was *too* skinny? I kept thinking of ways to leave. The door was right there. I could just get up and go. I heard my name called, and it jerked me out of my thoughts. As I walked towards the examining room, I decided to tell him everything I could about my situation and prayed that he would understand and offer me help. It was time to be honest, not just with the doctor, but with myself.

The words poured out of my mouth like a flood. I explained that I felt like I was too skinny, I felt grumpy, miserable, my tolerance was gone, and everything irritated me. I told him how I hardly ate any food at all and lived off coffee. I told him how I'd gone five months without really eating anything. The tears flowed, and I told him that I believed I was anorexic. The doctor listened to me without interrupting. I could tell he understood what I was saying. I was 98 pounds!

I was shocked when I saw the number. I had anxiety and felt like I was going to have a panic attack. I had horrible thoughts about what I'd done to myself. Was I going to die? Finally, a few days later, the doctor's office called and asked if I could review my tests with the doctor. He wanted to see me right away, which made me feel relieved that I would know what was happening, but also I panicked because, well, maybe I didn't want to really know. I was sad and confused by it all.

The results were not as bad as I had imagined they would be. The doctor thought there might be something wrong with my calcium levels and my iron, but generally, all was fine. He said that because I had milk in my coffee, that it may have helped my calcium levels and that the coffee had stopped me from passing out. Even with no food in my system, the caffeine kept me going. At that moment, I thanked God for coffee. The doctor sat down across from me and looked me in the eyes. He told me if I lost one more pound, I would end up in the hospital. He confirmed that my illness was anorexia. Hearing this confirmation felt like a weight lifted because I now knew the problem, and so now I could fix it. I could no longer live in denial, and it felt good.

The doctor told me he wanted me to go to meetings with other people who had eating disorders. I agreed to go to the meetings as I knew I needed to get help as I had three children, and they needed their mom. In the beginning, I was super nervous. I had no idea what to expect. The only way to explain it was that it was similar to an AA meeting where you introduce yourself. I had to stand up and say, "Hi, I'm Sheri, and I have an eating disorder." It was terrifying. I didn't go to the meetings for long. I didn't feel they were helping me. I made another doctor's appointment to discuss what other options might be available to me without going to the hospital. The doctor suggested that I see a psychiatrist. I thought, *oh no, not a head doctor*, but I agreed to go.

It wasn't that bad. I liked to talk and have conversations with others, so I thought I could handle it. The psychiatrist asked me to explain how I got to this point in my life. I explained that when I had my second child that I gained quite a bit of weight, and I kept trying to lose it, but it was almost impossible. The weight would not come off. Three years later, I went through a horrible separation and, at the same time, fell for one of my best friends. In my confused state, I thought that if I wanted a chance to be with him, I needed to lose weight.

I then went on to say that the stress of the situation, being a single mother, and looking for work caused me to lose weight fast. I felt like I looked great, and to my happy surprise, I even got the guy I wanted, even though we were more like "friends with benefits." He lived in Surrey, which wasn't too far from where I lived in New Westminster, and he came to see me all the time. I found a job, and a friend's sister babysat for me.

I was thankful that I found someone I could trust to look after my kids. It was tough, though, because I started working nights and had to take the kids to Surrey to stay the night with the sitter while I went to work in Burnaby and then back to Surrey to pick them up. My oldest child started kindergarten, and I had a three-year-old. I was worn out from not eating right and living on coffee. Then I noticed that my "friend with benefits" wasn't coming over very much.

Eventually, I got up the courage to ask him what was going on, and he told me that he didn't want to be with me. He wanted to date someone, but it wasn't me. I was devastated! Deep down, I always knew this would happen and that this day would come. I never spoke up about my feelings, but maybe if I did, things would have turned out differently. I guess I was worried if I said how I felt, our friendship would be ruined.

I ended up meeting someone else and had my third child in 1996. He was born premature, and so tiny. I believe it was because I was anorexic, and I was not eating well. A lot can happen to your body if you do not put proper nutrition into it. I became moody, and I was not thinking straight. I was not myself.

I told the psychiatrist my whole story. He suggested I take medication, but I asked what it was going to do. He told me it would help me get my appetite back. A year went by, and I didn't gain a pound. I ended up a size 0. I cried and was so discouraged. I knew I had to talk to the psychiatrist again to see if there was a different medication that I could take. He started me on a new drug, but it was another year until I finally began to gain some weight. I eventually noticed that I had a little muffin top, where your belly hangs over the top of your pants. I started thinking that I was looking pretty good. I began to feel better, mentally and physically. One day I bumped into a co-worker friend. She encouraged me to come back to work and said that I was needed. I agreed, and it turns out it was the best thing for me. To this day, I am very grateful to my friend Terry for encouraging me to return to work.

As life would happen, the years went on, and I ended up in another relationship that did not work out. We decided to separate. And wouldn't you know it, but my "friend with benefits" from years before contacted me and asked if we could be in a relationship again. I thought long and hard about it as I didn't want to go backward, but in the end, I decided to go for it. The first time we were young and stupid. Only time will tell if it was the right thing to do this time around.

I look back on my life and appreciate it all. The good things, the bad things, all of it. I am always aware of my need for food, to have energy, to be able to think straight, and to manage my mood swings. I am happy in my skin, and I now believe that I'm beautiful just the way God made me. And you know what? So are you.

**Sheri Sacco**

"Courage is the most important of all the virtues because without courage, you can't practice any other virtue consistently."

**MAYA ANGELOU**

# THIRTEEN

## Meet the Authors

*Vanessa Downer*

*Everybody Dies*

*But today is not my day*

Vanessa Downer : Born and raised in Vancouver, BC, Canada. Currently resides on Gabriola Island, BC, Canada. I am currently assisting my father in the day to day care of my mother, who has dementia and a type of Parkinson's disease.

I was involved in a number of local groups on the Island, but due to Covid and my Cancer, they have either been shut down (except virtually) or I am no longer physically able to participate.

I still do my crocheting for Christ Church Gabriola Prayer Shawl group. I love to crochet, and I am also making the shawls to eventually sell online. I cannot wait to get a virtual store up and running.

I have a dog and cat who keep me entertained for hours. I love Gabriola and enjoy exploring all the beaches and parks.

If you would like to reach me, I am available through vanessa.j.-downer@gmail.com or Instagram: gardenfairie63.

Thank you for your interest in my story, and it has not ended yet.

———

*Lynn Colman*

*Tales From an Expert Former Hider*

*How I kicked the hiding habit and learned how to speak up*

Lynn Coleman is an expert former hider, born in the UK and living in the Netherlands. She has two teenagers, two kittens, and too few hours in the day. After her degree in languages, Lynn's spent much of her life traveling and accumulating more languages as she goes; she speaks three languages fluently, another two well and can order tea and a sandwich in several others.

Lynn's business helps coaches, trainers and healers create and grow their online business. She supports them with tech, developing their offers, and finding the words to express what they do. She does that using a process she calls "listening with your heart."

Lynn's discovered that having the words to say what you want is one thing, daring to use them quite another. That's why she's decided to share her own, very personal story here. She wants to encourage other women to stop hiding. She believes that the world needs our warmth, our expertise, and our talents. It needs us to find our words and to speak up.

Lynn would be very happy to speak to you at:
https://yourepicbusiness.com
https://www.facebook.com/speakupsotheworldcanlisten
https://www.instagram.com/your.epic.business/

———

*Marisa Lavallee*

*The Cabin in the Woods*

*A young girl's story of survival in the wilderness*

Marisa Lavallee had a turbulent life, and because of a nervous breakdown at the age of 14, she left school. Thirteen years later, she returned and went on to get a business degree. She owned and managed a number of businesses.

In her thirties, she obtained her Real Estate license and enjoyed many successful years in the Real Estate Industry.

Marisa is now sixty-three and is the co-founder of Wet Coast Clothing. A unique women's clothing store located on beautiful Vancouver Island.

Marisa purchased a home on an acreage in a very rural area of Vancouver Island 16 years ago. This is where she enjoys her dogs, painting, and bird watching.

You can find Wet Coast Clothing on Facebook at https://www.facebook.com/Wet-Coast-Clothing-55698760106446 or if you'd like to reach out personally to her wetcoastclothing@gmail.com.

———

*Kim Beck*

*DAY ZERO*

*The day that changed my life April 10, 1987*

I am Kim Platis (legally, happily married to Bill since 2001) As for my work in real estate I am known as Kim Beck simply because I have been a realtor much longer that I have been Mrs. Platis, so I kept Beck for work and the odd occasion that I got to interact with my sons teachers or school during their time there.

I currently live in Cloverdale, British Columbia and I work serving the lower mainland.

I came to realize that I am not in the real estate business, I am in the experience business. That, in a very meaningful way, I get to bring change to the quality and direction of people's lives.

I have had this privilege since 1992 and have worked continuously with the Royal LePage Northstar office. When people ask what I do for a living, my response is, "I help people realize their dreams and then hand them the keys to it".

On a personal side, I am married to Bill and have two sons, Adam and Jordan. I have many interests from skiing, gold, watching football and biking. I was the the Alberta Freestyle ski team, taught skiing and was trained as a Canadian Ski Patrol.

Currently, I am a passionate supporter of BC Children's Hospital and Zajac Foundation and the Royal LePage Shelter Foundation.

Professionally, I have sold over 1200 homes in my career, worked with many developers selling land, lots, homes, townhomes, and condominiums. I own real estate in Canada and Arizona.
One of my favorite quotes comes from Franklin D Roosevelt...

*"Real estate cannot be lost or stolen, nor can it be carried away. Purchased with common sense, paid for in full, and managed with reasonable care, it is about the safest investment in the world."*

https://kimbeck.ca/
https://www.facebook.com/kim.platis

Kim Beck
Personal Real-Estate Corporation
Royal LePage Northstar
604-312-8369
Helping you since 1992

———

*Kandis Wells*

*A Love Letter to Myself*

*A path to forgiveness*

I grew up in a small town in Alberta, and being that small-town girl is still at the core of who I am today.

I've been blessed to live a diverse and exciting life, living all over North America and enjoying many different lifetimes within this one incredible lifetime.

I'm a mortgage broker, classically-trained French pastry chef, runner, and sometimes golfer.

I'm honored to be included in this group of women telling our stories. There is much to be discovered about ourselves through the lens of others' lives.

kandiswells.com
https://www.facebook.com/kandis12

———

*Leontine Boxem*

*Own Your Life to Become Finally Free*

*The woman who miraculously survived and learned what true freedom means*

I'm Leontine Boxem. I'm a divorced mother of 3 beautiful conscious children, cancer thriver, born in The Netherlands, living on this little magical island Ibiza (Spain) and working globally.

I'm a huge nature and watercolor painting lover. Nothing beats a good walk with fresh air in nature, looking to beautiful skies, mountains, and ocean - or the feeling of bright colors flowing over my paper, witnessing the paint dancing with the water.

**Free & Unstoppable**
As certified trainer and master life-coach, author and speaker - I help emphatic men and women who've already proved to be strong and resilient, to change perspective and see they don't have to work hard and prove more - to finally enter the stage where the 'good life', the joy and true connection is waiting for them.

When they come to me they feel lost, overwhelmed, there's something off… but they're ready to own their life, step into the light of their own story and find their unique voice. I help them to find their way to where they authentically live, lead and serve - so they become free and unstoppable as the best, empowered and most honest version of themselves!

My work is known for going deep without drama, a combination of a high dose realness with a high dose of love and true connection, and for the life changing experience. I can't wait to hear you and your story.

I offer support ranging from 3 weeks up to 12 months, it can be 1-

on-1 or group support, or a retreat on the beautiful island Ibiza (Spain, Europe).

More information & opportunity to work together:
www.leontineboxem.com
For speaking opportunities please contact me:
leontine@leontineboxem.com
Free Resources for you:
www.leontineboxem.com/free-resources
Join my free Free & Unstoppable Creators community:
www.facebook.com/groups/freeandunstoppablecreators

I love to connect to you! Send me a direct message and tell me what your biggest take away was by reading this book and my story!
www.instagram.com/leontineboxem
www.facebook.com/leontineboxem

**Conscious Cancer Club**
*EspECIFically for those who live with cancer, have survived cancer or have loved ones with cancer:*
Once a month I offer a free live online gathering called 'The Conscious Cancer Club circle'. You are welcome to join every first Sunday of the month at 19.30 CEST (Amsterdam, Ibiza). Check out www.timebuddy.com for your local time.
The sessions will be held inside my free group ww.facebook.-com/groups/freeandunstoppablecreators
More info & connection at
www.instagram.com/consious_cancer_club

———

*Michelle Den Boer*

*How I became the Mom to Moms*

*It takes a village to raise a kid... You are not alone.*

Michelle Den Boer is a Mom Mentor, Fitness/Wellness Coach, Inspirational Speaker, Author, and most important, a Mom. Her background as a Personal Trainer and motivation to help others become healthy drove her to lead her local community in a yearlong challenge to become healthier.

Throughout her life experience, she has realized that there are so many facets to life, and to be truly healthy, you have to work on all of them. One thing she knows for sure is being a mom is one of the most important jobs you can have, and it is a tough one. We as moms are raising someone's spouse, friend, co-worker etc, and in our determination of doing our best sometimes, it gets overwhelming, challenging, and rewarding.

However, we only have our kiddos for a short time before they head out into the world. Michelle has a belief in empowering your kids to make the right choice and let go of the power struggle. So, you can really enjoy your time with them.

Michelle has created a safe place where moms can come together and support one another, and mastermind troubles with each other. Her way of talking you through a challenge or feeling is one of unconditional support, trust, and believing that leads you to a conclusion without even realizing it. Join the Moms Nurturing Moms facebook group which is a great place to connect with Michelle and other like-minded moms. This is a place to share challenges, wins, and support each other.

Check out Michelle's free Empower Your Kids to Make the Right Choices which is where she shares some of her strategies, tools, and ideas in a free e-book.

**Connect with Michelle**
Social Media:
https://www.facebook.com/groups/367851997172163/

https://www.instagram.com/michelle_denboermom2moms/
Free E-book: Empower your kid to make the right choice
http://bit.ly/empoweryourkidsebook

———

*Shawna Roch*

*Finding Your Inner Power*

*You are the secret sauce*

I am a Mindset & Success Coach, Founder of Sexy Sales Goddess, Selling Your Way. I am passionate about helping female coaches, healers & entrepreneurs sell with confidence in a way that feels as easy as having a conversation.

I grew up in Edmonton, Alberta, and moved to Calgary, Alberta, in 1994, where I met and married my best friend. In 2005 we moved to a small Town called Black Diamond, Alberta, where we built our dream home on Diamond Crescent, and yes, I love diamonds. I am a momma to two fur babies and a wife of 20 years, I proposed to my husband 20 years ago on Valentine's Day, and we were married nine days later. On our 10th anniversary, ten of us few to Caba, San Lucas, where we renewed our vows on the beach. It was magical. As soon as we can get together as a group again, we will be renewing our vows for our 20th, in our backyard with the Marriage commissioner and friend who married us 20years ago. Bernie has been my rock, my support, and he believed in me no matter what.

I shared my story in hopes to inspire women. I thrived in an industry where I was up against all kinds of odds because I choose to do it my way. I knew I was the secret sauce.

I have been on my own transformation journey for the past three years and have fallen in love with the coaching industry. I am honored to bring together my 25 years of sales and marketing, combined with the past three years of experience and certifications, to help other women.

Website: www.shawnarochcoaching.com
Facebook Biz Page: www.facebook.com/shawnarochcoaching
Facebook Group: https://www.facebook.com/
groups/PowerhouseWomenWomenEmpoweringWomen/

———

***DanaGita Stratil***

***The Journey of Voice Awakening***

***How finding your voice can heal your life***

DanaGita Stratil is the founder of the Awakened Voice Academy, teaching healers, change-makers, and coaches how to free their true voice and unleash their creative expression. She has been a voice expert for over 35 years as a singer, performer, presentation skills coach, and intuitive voice healer.

Her expertise has come together to support others on their journey along their unique path to spiritual awakening. From her early years, she learned the profound impact speaking and singing can have. She has often suffered rejection and being shut up by people or traumatic experiences. After a severe health and life crisis, she found that her primary healing tool was, in fact, her own voice.

It has been the transformational power of sound that has helped her heal from all childhood trauma as well as grow spiritually. Each time she recovered from a life challenge, she gained deep insights and incredible voice and healing techniques.

DanaGita has studied and practiced multiple healing techniques and different singing styles. Her favorite voice expression includes mantras and chants, overtones, and Shamanic journeys. She performed as a solo artist and in different ensembles and with her own choir.

DanaGita actually means 'the gift of song' in Sanskrit. She understands the magic of this gift: awakening people to who they truly are. When they discover their authentic voice, they can speak or sing their unique, deep truths from a place of peace, love, and wisdom, just as she has learned how to do.

Born in the Czech Republic, DanaGita moved to Switzerland as a young girl. When she's not on one of her many journeys to spiritual sites around the globe, she can often be found hiking and singing in the Swiss Alps.

Explore your voice at www.danagita.com
Social media: https://www.facebook.com/danagitacom/

---

*Kelly Cross*

*I'll Never Be Like Them*

*Choosing my own future despite my past*

Writing my story has been challenging but rewarding at the same time. This is the first time I have ever written anything about my past, not even in a journal. I've only shared the stories in this book with a few close friends up until now.

After my stories in the book ends, I've gone on to live a wonderful life. In my twenties, I was single, had wonderful friends. I utilized this time to take some challenges and opportunities. Mom was still in the picture, but life outside of that was good. I've worked and managed businesses in several different industries doing different roles within them. Each one helped grow my knowledge and confidence in myself and business. Once I hit my thirties, life took another shift in focus. Working was no longer my main focus; I now have a family that needs me, loves me, and who I want to be with.

My life is so different and so much better than I ever thought possible. I've been with my husband, Paul, for 21 years now. We've grown together and built a family unlike any that I've ever experienced. We have two beautiful boys who are now 18 and 15; they're intelligent, kind, and incredible people. I've been blessed to be here to see our boys grow, change and experience all the possibilities open to them in their lives. About ten years ago, I was able to find my Aunt, my cousin, and his daughter. I hadn't seen them in about 40 years, and we've built a relationship that means so much to my family and me.

Now with the boys older, I've stepped back into a more active role. I am helping to build the companies that Paul and I have. I know my future holds more opportunities to explore, and we'll see where that may lead.

———

*Marie*

*Abandoned*

*One Response to Feeling Abandoned is to Abandon Yourself*

I grew up on the hillside of a small village, surrounded by mountains reaching as high as the eye can see. But like most younger people who live in remote areas, I craved the see the big city. So when I was just sixteen years old, I made my way to the UK and roomed with four other girls in a flat overlooking the city.

Painting was always a passion for me, and I spend many afternoons at the local park selling my artwork. I did well and found I was able to support myself while creating for myself and others.

I've flown a plane, traveled to Tibet and meditated with monks, and spent two months in Africa caring for orphaned elephants.

Now, I am contemplating taking my daughter and going back to the beautiful hillside community where I grew up. I believe my daughter will thrive there as I did.

From there, I don't' know what life will bring for myself and my daughter, but I am excited to discover what it will be. I am open to receive all the good things this amazing life has to offer.

————

**Sheri Saco**

**How My Mirror Saved MyLife**

**My battle with anorexia**

Writing my story was healing for me. I knew I had been holding onto my past, maybe feeling some shame, and keeping it pushed deep inside of me. Having the chance to put it on paper allowed me to realize that it wasn't my fault and there was nothing to feel shameful about. I'm so happy that I no longer feel that I need to hide, which is what shame does to a person.

I want you to know that if you are struggling with anorexia or any other kind of eating disorder, there is no shame, and you are not alone. And know that you are beautiful, inside and out.

I've had some great adventures in my life. I have gone skydiving, yes, I jumped out of a perfectly good plane. I feel I can conquer anything life throws at me. And I love going for walks and hiking.

I grew up in a tiny seaside community in British Columbia, Canada. I have raised my children, and now I enjoy spending time with my three grandchildren. I just love them like crazy. I'm very grateful for my children. They put up with the turmoil I put them through. To my children, I love you to the moon and back.

I would like to also tell you how much I appreciated my doctor; he was always listening to me. I was so nervous going to see him. He never judged me and was so supportive. Do not be afraid to reach out to health professionals. They are there to help.

My friends were there, standing by me. Not all my friends knew about my anorexia, but the ones that did know really stuck with me and supported me in many ways. Don't be afraid to let others into our life. Many will want to support you.

And I want to thank Julie for allowing me to write my story and allow me to heal by telling my story.

# FOURTEEN

# Meet Julie Fairhurst

I grew up in a highly hostile home environment. Alcoholism, emotional abuse, spousal violence, and poverty were rampant in my home as a child. It was a chaotic, stressful, and unstable place to grow up. If you have ever seen the television show called Shameless… well, that is precisely what my siblings and I grew up in.

I knew from the time I was a young child that I did not want to live this way. I do not know where it came from, but I knew it was wrong somewhere inside, and I wanted to do better. But how? How do you do better when you were never taught a different way.

Pregnant at 14 years of age, married at 17 and divorced at 29, a single mother with three young children, with a grade 8 education, I thought my life was set to failure, following down my parents' path. I was headed in the wrong direction.

But, somewhere deep inside, that young girl showed up and reminded me that I wanted better for my life. It wasn't easy. I had no support from anyone, not a soul. I had to do it all on my own.

Was it an easy road? No, it was far from easy. I was a single mom for 24 years. We lived off government handouts, and I stood in line at food banks to feed my kids. At Christmas, we received Christmas hampers, and I would go to the toy bank to get presents for the kids. The path we were on was not easy to change, especially when it is all that you know.

But I did it. I went back to school and finished my education. I built an outstanding sales career and won the companies top awards, and was the first woman to achieve top salesperson, year after year. I was able to buy a home on my own and provide a stable environment to raise my children in.

Some people would say they never looked back, but I do every day. Why? Because I never want to forget the journey that led me to where I am today. And today, my life is entirely different. I didn't just fall into this new life. I worked at it, every day, all the time.

I now help others who are struggling in their lives. They may be living in poverty. They may have a negative view of themselves and an unhealthy mindset. They may be struggling in their career and feel lost. Just like I did.

If you would like to reach out to me for any reason, I would love to connect with you. Here is how you can find me.

Wishing for you to be able to live your best life, the life you came here to live.

**You can find me at:**
www.rockstarstrategies.com
www.juliefairhurst.com

**Follow me on social media:**
Facebook: Rock Star Strategies
www.facebook.com/juliefairhurstcoaching
Instagram: Inspire by Julie
www.instagram.com/inspirebyjulie
LinkedIn

www.linkedin.com/in/rockstarstrategies/

**Looking for Julie's books or free resources?**
Look here: https://rockstarstrategies.com/resources/
https://rockstarstrategies.com/work-with- me/

**Julie's Books on Amazon**
https://www.amazon.ca/s?k=julie+fairhurst&ref=nb_sb_noss

**Follow my blog**: https://rockstarstrategies.com/blog/

# Other Books by Julie Fairhurst

- Women Like Me: A Celebration of Courage and Triumphs
- Your Mindset Matters
- Revealing a New You: The 7 point Attitude Adjustment That Will Change Your Life
- Dignity: 10 Steps to Build Your Self-Worth
- Self Esteem Confidence Journal
- Build Your Self Esteem: 100 Tips designed to boost your confidence
- Agent Etiquette:14 Things You Didn't Learn in Real Estate School
- 7 Keys to Success: How to Become a Real Estate Sales Badass
- 30 Days To Real Estate Action
- Net Marketing

## Acknowledgments

*Thank you!*

**To the 12 Authors in this volume of Women Like Me**

My dearest authors, you were all incredible to work with. When you were stuck, you asked for help, you didn't stay stuck, nor did you quit. I know there were a few of you who considered quitting while writing your story. It takes bravery to open yourself up to the world and tell your story. And, you didn't quit! I am celebrating each one of you for stepping up and digging deep into your past. I know it was challenging to go there, but you did it. You got your story out of your head, onto paper, and into the book.

Our past can imprison us. Even if it was ten years ago or 50 years ago, we are still held prisoner, unable to break free. Telling your stories is an emotional release, and with that release comes freedom.

Thank you from the bottom of my heart, ladies. Not only have you all grown, but I have as well. Thank you for trusting me with your personal stories and being willing to have them published in

Women Like Me. And most of all, thank you for helping others who may be unable to live their best lives because they are a prisoner of their past. Through your stories, they may find acceptance and ultimately freedom.

**Jennifer Sparks – Amazon Bestselling Author, Speaker, and Self-Publishing Coach**

Jen is someone you want in your corner if you're going to write a book or learn how to be self-published. Her knowledge is outstanding in the publishing arena. Jen was always there for any questions I had and was a guide for getting Women Like Me published. I am incredibly grateful to have been able to work with Jen and look forward to working with her on more publishing projects.

If you have ever thought about writing a book of your own, be sure to reach out to Jen…

jennysparks@hotmail.ca
https://jennifersparks.ca/
http://www.stokepublishing.com/
https://www.facebook.com/jennifersparks.ca
https://www.instagram.com/jennifersparks.inspirethefire/
https://www.instagram.com/stokepub/

**Rob Breaks – My Rock**

I have to include my husband in these acknowledgments, for without him, none of my books may have ever been written or published. Rob, you were always there to support me and encouraged me along the way. It is crucial to have someone believe in you, especially when you are sailing into unknown waters. Rob, you are that person for me. Thank you for always believing in me, even when I did not believe in myself. You mean the world to me. I'm so grateful for you in my corner.

**To all of you who are reading Women Like Me**

Thank you for your support. It means so much to the authors and myself. As you may imagine, writing about your personal life story can be a daunting task. Many emotions rise to the surface during the process. The women who write in these books are brave souls who know how important it is to deal with past issues to be free.

It was also essential for the writers to pass along their life lessons to the reader. In that way, they hope to help you, the reader, heal from a past that may be holding you back.

Thank you once again for supporting all of us while we go through our journeys.

# Want to be a Women Like Me Author?

Do you have a story that needs to be told?
A story that is holding you back from living your best life?

We only get one chance. Our life is not a dress rehearsal for our
next lifetime.
We get one life, and it's here and now.

Don't allow the past to hold you back from your dreams, goals, love,
and success. If you feel like a prisoner of your past, then it's time to
break free of it and move on. There are many ways that can happen
for you.
I choose to free myself through writing.

Writing is therapeutic to the soul. Writing about your past events
can be beneficial, both emotionally and physically. You can increase
your feelings of well-being and even enhance your immune system!

If you'd like to take this journey with me, and other like-minded
women, then reach out to me.

Want to be a Women Like Me Author?

I can be reached at
julie@rockstarstrategies.com
or through my website
https://rockstarstrategies.com/contact/
I'm looking forward to meeting you.

All the best
Julie

Manufactured by Amazon.ca
Bolton, ON

19252117R00102